GREECE

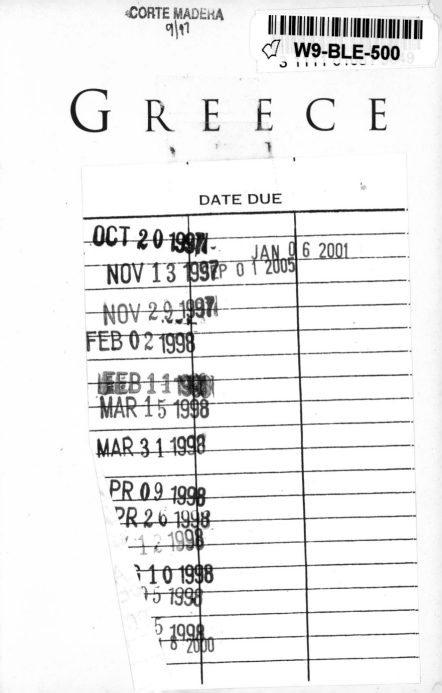

GOOD STORIES REVEAL as much, or more, about a locale as any map or guidebook. Whereabouts Press is dedicated to publishing books that will enlighten a traveler to the soul of a place. By bringing a country's stories to the English-speaking reader, we hope to convey its culture through literature. Books from Whereabouts Press are essential companions for the curious traveler, and for the person who appreciates how fine writing enhances one's experiences in the world.

"Coming newly into Spanish, I lacked two essentials —a childhood in the language, which I could never acquire, and a sense of its literature, which I could."

—Alastair Reid, *Whereabouts: Notes on Being a Foreigner*

OTHER TRAVELER'S LITERARY COMPANIONS

Costa Rica edited by Barbara Ras
with a foreword by Oscar Arias

Prague edited by Paul Wilson

Vietnam edited by John Balaban
and Nguyen Qui Duc

Israel edited by Michael Gluzman and Naomi Seidman
with a foreword by Robert Alter

Australia edited by Robert Ross
available October 1997

GREECE

A TRAVELER'S LITERARY COMPANION

EDITED BY

ARTEMIS LEONTIS

WHEREABOUTS PRESS
SAN FRANCISCO

Published in the United States by
Whereabouts Press
2219 Clement Street, Suite 18
San Francisco, California 94121

Distributed to the trade by
Consortium Book Sales & Distribution

Map of Greece by Bill Nelson

Manufactured in the United States of America
on recycled paper.

Library of Congress Cataloging-in-Publication Data

Greece: a traveler's literary companion /edited by Artemis Leontis
     p.   cm. (Traveler's literary companions)
  ISBN 1-883513-04-9 (alk. paper)
  1. Greek fiction. Modern—20th century—Translations into
English.   2. Greece—fiction.   I. Leontis, Artemis.   II. Series.
PA5296.E5G74   1997
889.3'308—dctk
                                                    97–13267
                                                    CIP

5   4   3   2   1

Contents

Preface

A WORLD UNKNOWN to most visitors to Greece comes
alive in the pages of these stories. The landscape may be
familiar—a superb canvas of mountains, beaches, villages,
cities, and ruins, all bathed in the rich light of the
Mediterranean—but here nothing is idyllic. Time has not
stopped. Everything is moving. The scene is of a world in
inexorable change. War, civil strife, and foreign occupation
disrupt peace; urbanization, modernization, and tourism
bring excitement and confusion. Against these forces, the
protagonists of the stories try valiantly to find stable
ground. Their strength is their ingenuity, the humor and
mythmaking gifts they foster as they respond to volatile
times. More than any of these characteristics, their perspective of the long duration prevails. Their Greece is not
a finished product to be captured by the casual snapshot.
It is a world still becoming, best understood when one
moves with the dynamic, stirring drama that comprises
just one moment in an unfinished story.

This book offers a fresh approach to Greece, a tall order
since Greece is a country thoroughly labeled by foreign
travelers' accounts. One wonders, is there a single untried

path through Athens, Delphi, Olympia, Mycenae, or any other famous site that has inspired centuries of travel? No book has ever introduced Greece exclusively through modern Greek prose. It is astonishing that no guidebook for travelers, many of whom are eager to circumvent the commonplace and reach unfamiliar ground, has ever followed a contemporary Greek approach to Greece. Yet ours is an age that has come to appreciate the lessons of our contemporaries as well as of those long dead. If Homer, Sappho, Euripides, and Plato live on as household names, isn't it time to read Seferis and Elytis, two Nobel laureates; Kazantzakis, Venezis, Vassilikos, and Karapanou, whose works have existed in English translation for several decades; Papadopoulou, Axioti, Zenakos, and Faïs, who appear in English here for the first time? Ancient authors opened a wide door into Greece. New generations of authors now stand there, offering us an engrossing view of a modern world much closer to our own sensibilities.

The rewards are rich for the reader of modern Greek prose. Greek literature draws freely from every period of its long oral and written evolution. It is not just the classical tradition that finds its way into these stories. Authors freely mix histories that are personal and monumental, oral and written, modern and ancient. Strong feelings of allegiance bind individual works to the village, town, or region regarded as the real homeland—what Greeks refer to as their *topos*. Moreover, Greeks have a personal stake in this topos. The strong connection of literature to place will move anyone who recognizes Greece as a modern country that continues to refashion itself—rather than an old cultural idea vaguely responsible for the development of poetry, drama, philosophy, rhetoric, democracy, and science in the West.

The adventurous reader will jump at the prospect of traveling into this unfamiliar territory. The odyssey through mountainous terrain of site-specific narrative to faraway accounts of the struggle for dignity and self-sufficiency is long and unhurried, full of adventure and experiences, I have discovered. My own journeys to Greece have been richly enhanced by a lifetime commitment to the study of Greek letters. I have traveled through the Peloponnese with Kazantzakis in hand. Ioannou has been my guide to Thessaloniki; Hatzis and Milionis opened doors to Epirus, Seferis to Delphi, Axioti to Mykonos, and Hakkas to Athens—perhaps the most difficult but ultimately rewarding city. I have been surprised by the diversity of peoples: gypsies, Armenians, Jews, Pomuks, Turks, Vlachs, Sarakatsans, expatriate Americans, Muslims, Catholics, Greek Orthodox, and people of specific regional identifications fill the pages of this anthology. I have been disturbed by the great forces of change that set the drama in motion: incoming waves of refugees, mass emigration, decades of war, civil strife, foreign occupations, and the peaceful invasions of tourism and consumer culture. I have been inspired by the many creative, dignified responses to violent destruction: strategies of forgetting, rituals of remembrance—none more moving than in Xexakis's "Smile from the Abyss." And I have been entertained by the rapid, endless flow of language that animates so many stories, from Vassilikos's "The White Bear" to Chouliaras's "America Is No Longer Here."

In many works, the besieged center of stability is itself

the protagonist. Traditional social codes, time-honored
rites, the Sisyphean struggle to make the Greek economy
self-sufficient, memories of other homelands—all are at
the heart of many stories that tell of sudden changes that
divide people or bring them suddenly face to face. After
the exchange of populations in 1922, both Greek and
Turkish people lost a way of life that gave them distinction, as Venezis's "Mycenae" and Alexiou's "Fountain of
Brahim-Baba" attest. Faïs's "Autobiography of a Book" reminds us that in the course of a few weeks in 1943,
Germans led the Jewish population of Thrace en masse to
its destruction, while Muslim women clattered tin and
copper utensils to fend off the Bulgarian occupation.
Other groups have been yielding gradually to the forces of
assimilation. Today the pageantry of passing camel caravans sounds like myth rather than history. Even more than
World War II, the Greek Civil War (1945–49) created
dramatic situations, as the refuge of the village home became a place of danger from which people were obliged to
flee. From 1950 to 1985 half of Greece become Athenian,
and Athens's underclass neighborhoods like Kaisariani, so
colorfully depicted in Hakkas's "Fresco," began to blend
into the invasive sameness of the sprawling modern city.

In choosing stories for this anthology, a process that
gave me the pleasure of revisiting so many stories that
could have filled so many more volumes, I have adhered to
several criteria. First, I tried to find good stories, some immediately accessible, others taking the form of an essay
with several narratives, or a modernist story that engages
the reader in a game of catching the referent, or a chronicle that retells local history through narratives and dialogue with a deeper resonance. Second, there were

site-specific considerations. I worked hard to touch as many geographical regions of Greece as possible. I also aimed to represent the range of Greek worlds I know, from ancient sites to places of significance in recent history: cities, towns, villages, islands that have undergone startling, disempowering changes during this century, and the lost or newly adopted homelands of succeeding Greek diasporas.

Last, I wanted to make available as many newly translated works as possible. Collections of Greek stories in English are scarce. This is a rare opportunity to introduce readers to prose pieces previously unpublished outside Greece. I would not have been able to manage this had I not found translators willing to work quickly for small rewards. Good translators are precious gems. I thank all the translators with whom I worked closely for their skill, speed, patience, goodwill, and advice: Yiorgos Anagnostu, Jane Assimakopoulos, Alison Cadbury, John Chioles, Cynthia Hohlfelder, Gail Holst-Warhaft, Gerasimus Katsan, Helen Dendrinou Kolias, Anastasia Koumidou, Yianna Liatsos, Catherine Siskron, and Karen Van Dyck. Authors Yiorgos Chouliaras, Michel Faïs, Rhea Galanaki, Christoforos Milionis, and Leonidas Zenakos were especially cooperative. I also thank Yianna Athanasatou, Claudio Fogu, Victoria Holbrook, Peter Murphy, Maria Mylonas, Andreas Kitsos-Mylonas, and Martha Klironomou for their help, Roland Moore for his tip, Julian Anderson for her invaluable editorial advice, and Vassilis Lambropoulos, an endless source of humor and knowledge. This book is dedicated to Daphne Lambropoulos, for her patience and inspiration.

—*Artemis Leontis*

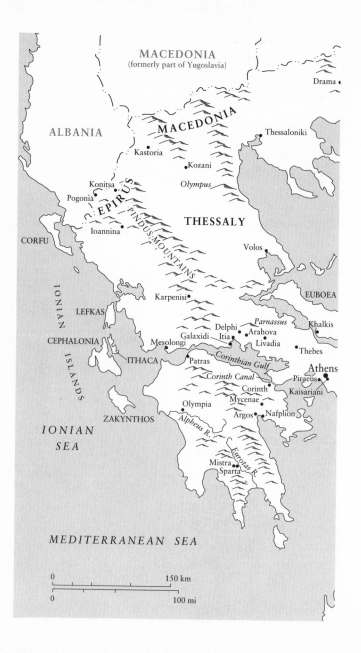

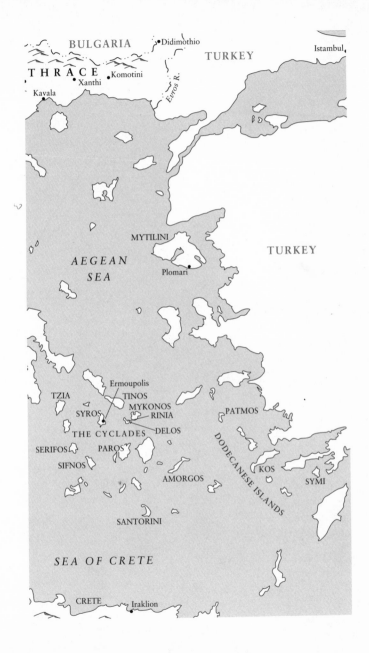

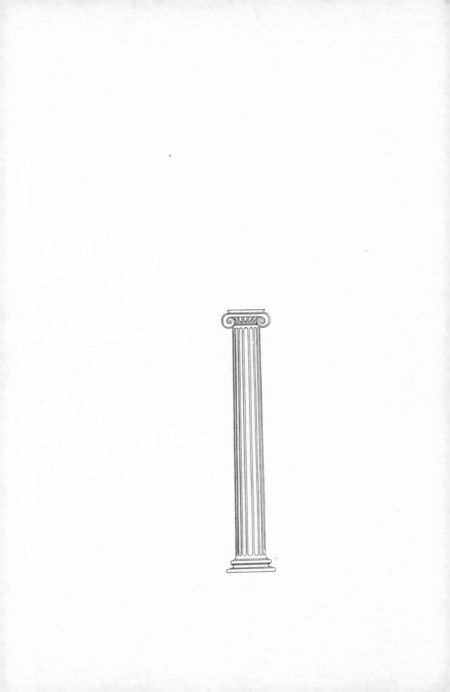

The White Bear

Vassilis Vassilikos

The idea of a novel cut me like a knife . . .
Mentally, I was killing a bear.
—Yiannis Skaribas, *Figaro's Solo*

I. HOW A WHITE BEAR ENDED UP IN ATHENS

THE WHITE BEAR was wandering around the streets of Athens, searching for its lost master.

Who is this white bear? Who is its lost master? That is the topic of our story today.

But let's start with some background information. Which Athens was it wandering around? What did Athens of that period look like? That period of crisis, of inflation, of renewed devaluation.

Do economic terms, terms that are detached from the action and the character of its heroes, have their place in a story? What is the difference between the myth and the mythified?

All questions that demand an answer. But we, readers, are not about to mythologize. We are enlisted in the struggle for a better tomorrow for the world and for ourselves, we are fighting for better days to come. And they are bound to come, there's no doubt about that. All bodes well in this better-than-all-possible worlds.

But before we even start, we have to obey a narrative convention that wants the bear to be of neutral gender, because since childhood we are used to referring to a bear as "it," unless it is specified as a Papa or a Mama bear. In any case, we have no other choice but to work with the materials available. And these materials are, for the most part, determined by chance.

Let us not try to make head or tail of something that has neither. If we had an organized life, a timetable, a position that gave us precise authorities, whether constitutionally guaranteed or not, we might proceed according to a gradual, well-thought-out method. But when everything is on the verge of chaos, when everything marches on in the dark (inside power, in the center of its center, in its main core, there is a dark nucleus), everything is possible, every beginning is good, nobody is forcing anyone: I am not forced to tell the story of the bear that got lost in Athens during the holidays, nor you, much less you, reader, to listen to this story, which, alas, is in danger of becoming a boomerang coming back to hit me in the gut, making me, once again, throw up all the disgust and joy I get from life.

The important thing is that, up to this moment when I am sitting down to write, even though I smoke a lot, I have yet to suffer a heart attack, which would scare me and make me give up or cut down on my smoking, roll up my sleeves, and start writing only about the important events of my life, leaving a sort of heritage testament to posterity. I am still now (knock wood) perfectly healthy. I have not burdened others with insurmountable worries. When Aliki and I broke up, we both cried a little, of course, but this took place within reasonable, human limits. She flew off to stay with a friend to alleviate her solitude, while I buried myself in the anonymous crowd that was traveling by plane, in order to retire into my own solitude. Of course, I am still damp from Aliki's touch, from her virginal freshness against my cheek, her lust for life that nothing could injure. I think of her, I want her; that girl tore me to pieces. I'm like a schoolboy when I'm with her, but I like this state she often put me in.

On the whole, therefore, I am well. Amid the general misery of my country and my people, I am still behaving relatively optimistically. Proof of that being that I'm still in the mood to type. The required amount is at least three pages a day. Let us get to three pages to start with, and then we can move painlessly to five, eight, sometimes even ten, on those days when inspiration fills my sails, a wind that tears itself against the riggings and masts, a nor'wester, as it's called. A moment will arrive, during this digging up of feelings, when I will identify with the universe, with the deeper path of life, when I will surpass myself, and then, as gambling people say, I will have hit the jackpot. I will feel like a writer worthy of his mission. But until then I must walk a long, joyless, monotonous road, overgrown with nettles and thorns. The peaks are few. And precarious. And the road that leads to them seems interminably long!

It was from such a peak that our friend the bear descended. It had been living free in the mountain when its lair was discovered by some topographers who were taking measurements for the digging of a tunnel through the mountain—that of Ahladokambos, to be precise—in order to shorten the road leading into the interior of the Mani. They took the bear and brought it to the town of Kalamata. That way, while it was still a cub, the bear associated with people and came to know their peculiarities. It lived as a domesticated animal until the day when, the daughter of the topographer having gotten involved with a Gypsy (the one who had relieved her of the little gold chain around her ankle), the young bohemian spoke to his father about a bear that lived, if you please, in the backyard of his girlfriend's house. The Gypsy's father went and asked the girl's father not for his daughter, but for his bear. In order to sell, the topographer would have to get permission from his daughter, who had become attached to the animal. His daughter, Aliki from Kalamata (four *a*'s in a row: Kavála has but three; Patras, two; and Tziá, a single one), in accordance with her friend the switch-hitter, told her daddy that he could give the bear to the man who wanted to buy it. The young Gypsy who was turning her on had made this a condition of their love affair continuing.

The topographer was gladly rid of the animal, which had caused all kinds of problems in his garden and had made him the laughingstock of the neighborhood. One neighbor in particular, Manolis from America, had suffered an accident in Chicago and was not all there, poor man. Every time Manolis saw the topographer, whether in the street or the café, Manolis would ask him, at the top of his voice, how his bear was doing.

And so it was that, from the mountain heights of Ahladokambos, after a brief sojourn in Kalamata, the bear found itself in the hands of the Gypsy, who took it to Athens for the Christmas holidays, obeying that ancient custom that dictates that Gypsies with bears should wander through various neighborhoods collecting money by making the bear do certain tricks. Now, how the bear came to get lost in the concrete city of Athens and how it was picked up by the traffic policeman at the junction of Third of September and Alkouli Streets and handed over to Police Lieutenant Livreas, we will see presently.

But first, a few words on the sexual attraction between Aliki and the young Gypsy who had relieved her of the small gold ankle chain; and a few words also on the consequences that the disappearance of the bear might well have had on the cultural life of Kalamata.

I should point out that it is purely coincidental that the young girl in our story has the same name as my friend, from whom I am expecting a tender phone call at any moment. It is one of those coincidences that occur both in life and in fiction. Nothing more. No further symbolism or thought association intended. Aliki from Kalamata is a high school senior with an acne-covered face. She goes to the cafés in town, where she sees the boys sitting around talking about motorbikes and soccer, but she avoids coming in contact with them.

On the outskirts of Kalamata, as almost everywhere in Greece, lies a semipermanent Gypsy camp, which provides the town with vegetables, Nissan pickups, seafood, fortune-tellers, witches, songs by Manolis Angelopoulos and Jehovah's Witnesses. As she strolled by the cafés with their plastic chairs and ice coffees, and the discos with their video clips, the young Aliki had decided to strike back at her *acne vulgaris* and cure it—something no dermatologist had succeeded in doing so far—by surrendering to a vulgar entanglement with the young Gypsy. This assignation took place one evening that May as her grandmother was in the garden, killing a chicken for the feast day of saints Constantine and Helen, which also happened to be the names of Aliki's father and mother. The young Gypsy was stealing plums when Aliki saw him and said: "Wait, you don't have to steal them. I'll give them to you." The Gypsy couldn't have asked for more. The household seemed like a privileged one. Aliki gathered lots of plums in her apron and took them to him just as the chicken fluttered in the old woman's hands, breathing its last. As she lifted her skirt, the Gypsy saw Aliki's pretty legs and became flustered. Twilight was falling, nobody could see them. Thus it came about that, amid the intoxicating fragrances of spring, Aliki gave him the gift of her first sigh, her first spasm, that coincided with the chicken's last one. From then on, every evening at six o'clock sharp, at the bottom of the garden, she would meet her friend, who was in no danger of compromising her in the café where her friends hung out, since Gypsies were not allowed inside. Besides, her swarthy lover was very sexy.

It was during that summer that her father, Constantine, who had a thick mustache and was a militant supporter of the Socialist Party, was awarded the contract for the digging of the tunnel that would shorten the national road between Athens and Kalamata by two whole hours and, having come across the white bear in the mountains, had brought it home as a gift to his daughter. And it was during the same summer that the young Gypsy, fancying the idea of a bear, had spoken about it to his father, the chief of the Gypsy camp. All of which led to the bear, aged only a few months, walking around Athens during the Christmas holidays.

As for the cultural life of Kalamata, no, the bear was not missed at all: a very active mayor had turned this town into a little Paris.

On the other hand, the bear had been something of a consolation in Athens, first cultural capital of Europe, until the moment when it got lost at the junction of Third of September and Alkouli Streets and put itself obediently into the hands of the police officer, who led it, according to regulations, to the traffic police headquarters nearby on Saint Constantine Street, as the bear had been obstructing traffic. The usual circulation restrictions in the center of town had been lifted because of the holidays, and the traffic was absolute chaos.

2. WHEREUPON IN ATHENS, FIRST CULTURAL CAPITAL OF EUROPE, THE SIGHT OF A WHITE BEAR STILL DRAWS PEOPLE'S ATTENTION

We are not among those who doubt that whatever was done was done well. However, our Gypsy started off from Kalamata in his Nissan pickup with Aliki the bear tied on the flatbed amid wishes for a bon voyage; like another Zampano, he took his own Strada. He made his first stop in Nafplion, first capital of the modern Greek state, before Athens. The summer Lotharios were resting up in the wintry square below the fortress of Palamidi, listening to the latest Harry Klynn* tape at full blast. The sight of the bear excited them. At Corinth Canal, where he stopped next, everybody was eating souvlaki and listening to the same

* Greek comedian. *Trans.*

tape. The Gypsy listened carefully to find out what people were laughing at. He heard about how different politicians acted in Parliament, about soccer players, and about well-known entertainers. During the next few days he taught all these things to his bear, who would mimic them with an acting talent as great as, if not greater than, that of the movie star who was also called Aliki. The bear would mimic the top Socialist minister speaking in Parliament, the goalkeeper Sarganis diving to save the ball, and the president of the republic embracing his wife.

Having thus trained his prize pupil, he would set out from working-class neighborhoods and march upon suburbs where, the summer before, the culture hounds had flocked in their Mercedeses to converted quarries to attend performances by Peter Brook and Peter Stein. These events had been successful beyond expectation. Children gathered round the Gypsy and the bear; so did grown-ups who hadn't seen such an old-fashioned spectacle in a long time. The Gypsy was raking it in. The poor man dreamed of sending his own son to school, so that he might escape the wretchedness to which society would condemn him for being the son of a Gypsy. The people laughed at Aliki's antics, and with the holidays drawing closer, having spent their Christmas bonuses, they amused themselves by watching the bear make fun of the neo-Hellene who was forced to tighten his belt, when for him a big gut had always been synonymous with prosperity. This act was not part of Harry Klynn's tape, which had been recorded before the devaluation of the drachma; the Gypsy had added it at the urging of a greengrocer friend of his.

At which point he decided to march up to the more distant suburbs to the east. However, although on the map this journey looked simple, in reality most roads were closed due to the digging of sewers. Just as it was in Kalamata. However, he made a decent living, thanks be to God, and had nothing to complain about. Not like when he was a boy and he had to sell flowers in the taverns. He even appeared on a TV show about occupations that were dying out, in which he said that his bear made the most money at the lines formed by the unfortunate Athenians waiting for a bus or a trolley. As he spoke, his gold teeth shone on the TV screen like a corporeal treasure.

3. WHEREUPON A GANG OF JUNKIES DECIDES TO DOPE UP THE GYPSY'S BEAR

They were just sitting around doing nothing. Each one had become the other's snitch. One would pretend to be friends with the other until he could squeal on him to score a hit. Nothing else counted in their relationships. Although relationships, the way most people perceive them, did not exist among them. Their only reason for living was to score a hit. The area was perfect for it, because of all the retired military officers. There were no cafés, no pool halls like one would find in other neighborhoods. There were no political party youth organizations, not even any kiosks. In other words, there was nothing reminiscent of a traditional suburban neighborhood with its video rental shops and funeral parlors open all night.

Here in Papagos there was nothing. Only wide roads where solitary types walked their dogs, where Filipino housemaids and gardeners pruned the trees at a distance from one another. The kids growing up here had nothing better to do than commit the odd burglary, siphon gas out of cars, and harass the local cops, who gave them the same fossilized bullshit as their parents. The appearance of the Gypsy and his bear could only cause their pinball brains to tilt. They convened and decided to drug the bear. The leader of the gang, son of the "Commie-eating" General Vorias and a former prison inmate (a fact that rendered his power over the others indisputable), suggested they first daze the animal with their motorbikes, irritating its master, and then, when the Gypsy wasn't looking, slip the bear a spiked pastry.

But the clever bear did not fall for this trap. To begin with, it had not liked this area, because it was full of barking guard dogs. Then the bear had looked into the eyes of those young people as they surrounded it. It searched for those dreamy eyes that would gaze at the bear in order to escape the misery of their lives, eyes that Aliki had often come across in the center of Athens, on the faces of passersby who held two or three plastic shopping bags; but here it did not find the eyes it was seeking. As a result, the bear showed no interest whatsoever in the pastry it was offered, while its master the Gypsy, thinking he had hit on an aristocratic neighborhood, passed the hat around, only to collect stones and dried shit. They even slit one of his truck tires, and he had to change it in the freezing cold. He left, cursing and swearing, while the junkies, furious that their devilish scheme had fallen through, followed him, revving wildly and popping wheelies, all the way to the suburb limits on Mesoghion Avenue.

4. AT TRAFFIC POLICE HEADQUARTERS

The officer on duty, Lieutenant Livreas, was taking a statement from a lady, Doña Rosita, who had just escaped death in a car crash at the junction of Mesoghion Avenue and Hypoxinou Street, when the traffic policeman came into his drab office to report the arrest of a stray bear. Next to the lieutenant sat a young traffic policewoman, who seemed to find the story amusing. "A bear found unaccompanied in the center of Athens? That's a good one." Lieutenant Livreas looked up from the lady's statement and asked the officer where he had put the bear.

"In the basement, Lieutenant," he replied. "We're waiting for its owner to come and claim it."

"It'll probably be a Gypsy," said the lieutenant, and turned his attention back to the lady, who was still shaken by her nighttime collision. In his head, he was trying to figure out where the hell this Hypoxinou Street was; he had never heard of it. He concluded that it must be a side street, in which case the lady who had been driving along Mesoghion Avenue had had the right-of-way and therefore the person who had crashed into her was solely to blame.

"But there wasn't just one, Lieutenant," insisted the woman. "Two cars crashed into me."

"Two? What do you mean, two?" the officer asked, puzzled.

"I told you: I slowed down, I flashed my headlights at them to show that I would keep going since I had the right-of-way, and even though I saw they had stopped, suddenly, I don't know why, they both crashed into me."

Lieutenant Livreas was hunched over his report, trying

to summarize the statement of the beautiful Doña Rosita in the conventional language of police reports, when the lottery ticket salesman walked into the office, his pole covered in tickets like a leafy tree. Both Livreas and his secretary berated him for their bad luck at the big New Year's drawing and refused to buy new tickets.

"What are we going to do with the bear?" asked the officer for the last time.

"Bring it here," said Livreas, sounding official.

"But it won't fit in the elevator."

"Then bring it up the back stairs."

The officer left the room.

"Were you serious, sir?" asked his secretary, as she stood up to welcome some colleagues wearing civilian clothes who had come to announce the glad tiding that they were finally leaving work.

Meanwhile, the officer went down to the basement, took the bear by its chain, and started to lead it up the stairs, but on the first floor he ran into an unusual congregation of young motorcyclists, probably motorcycle messengers who had been forced, because of a new law, to re-register their bikes. The hallway was packed solid outside the registry office, but the appearance of the white bear had a catalytic effect. Where it had been impossible to get through, panic and terror soon opened a space; the officer and his animal passed through easily and continued up the stairs. Both officers and civilians laughed at the unusual spectacle; the bear, who had never been in a public building before, did not seem perturbed by anyone or anything. Upon arriving at last at the lieutenant's office, the bear came face to face with its boss, the Gypsy, who threw himself on it sobbing woefully, like a poor man who has lost his sole possession. Unmoved by this display, the bear sat down and proceeded to follow what was being said about it, as if the discussion concerned another: Did the bear have a license to circulate? Had the Gypsy paid for a bear registration? Had the bear been cleared through customs? Since the bear had been imported, it must go through customs. The Gypsy thought he was losing his mind.

"It's from Ahladokambos, Lieutenant, it's not imported. This country has bears, doesn't it?"

"Bears come from the Soviet Union, from up north," the white bear heard one man say.

"It's Greek," insisted the Gypsy master. "Come on, Aliki, show them what the Socialists do in Parliament."

And so, while the office filled up with more and more policemen, the bear did its usual routine, then it pretended it was a goalkeeper diving for the ball—it didn't dive as far as it should have, of course, because the space was limited, but in its desperate attempt to prove it was Greek, it did whatever it could.

"And how come it got away?" insisted the lieutenant.

"I had gone, with all due respect, Lieutenant, to relieve myself. I left the bear outside the municipal rest rooms, and when I came back out it was gone."

"Okay, get going," said the commissioner as he marched into the office. He had heard that there was a bear in the building and was afraid the tabloids would get wind of it. "Get lost!"

The Gypsy, glad to have avoided a bureaucratic odyssey, declared he would take better care of the animal, took it by the chain, and walked out. Outside on the street, he breathed with relief. "You better not disappear on me again, you fleabag, or I'll wring your neck."

5. BUT WHERE DO I FIT INTO THIS STORY?

I bought Aliki the bear from the Gypsy at a disgracefully low price. He had wanted to get rid of the animal as soon as the holidays were over. He could no longer afford to feed it. This suited me fine, since I lived in a small villa in Halandri with a garden and I wanted company. In this house lived people who had nothing to do with me—in a way I was putting them up by default—and I wanted to have an animal of my own, since I didn't have a person of my own, or rather since I didn't want to have one. People generally have a lot of problems, whereas animals only give you their devotion and love. At night, I would take the bear to my room and we would sleep side by side. I always intentionally present it as my companion.

All it needed was a few caresses. It loved me very much. It would look into my eyes, its eyes concealing the unknown land of its origin. And I would dream of arctic steppes or distant retreats where man had never set foot.

In any case, when you circulate with a bear, just like with a dog, you discover things that were not evident at first. Many places are forbidden to you, and moving around in general becomes difficult. An animal, of whatever kind, imposes upon you the circle of a powerful spotlight. You cannot go unnoticed. People in the street will stop and stare. Women and children are fearful. They react atavistically to the sight of the animal that, very long ago, was their enemy.

During winter the bear did not suffer. But in the summer it seemed to have trouble with the heat. So I decided I would take my vacation time. I was going to show the bear Greece, but a Greece different from the one it had seen with its old master, the Gypsy. "Tomorrow we leave for Nafplion," I announced one morning as I awoke.

It had been years since I had been to Nafplion, and I was amused at the thought of returning and seeing all my old acquaintances, accompanied by a bear. So we got into my Toyota. At the tollgate, I got my first snide remark. The bear was sitting next to me in the passenger seat, with its seat belt tightly fastened, perfectly behaved, and ignoring the mustachioed man who looked over at it mockingly as he handed me my receipt. At Corinth Canal I fed it ten souvlaki, and from there we went straight to the new Xenia Hotel in Nafplion. I requested a room for two. Fortunately, there was one available.

"Two beds?"

"No, one double."

But at that moment, the kids who had been playing outside came in and got scared when they saw the bear. So did the clerk at the front desk. He was just about to say, "It is not allowed," when he recognized in me the former general secretary of the Greek Tourist Organization. He immediately notified the manager, whom, by a strange coincidence, I had appointed to this post before going into the army to do my military service. "I understand your situation," I said, "but there's not going to be a problem. The new cable car elevator goes directly to my room." That way, I wouldn't even pass through the hotel.

The bear was very happy with all this luxury. Later, we went for a walk on the back side of the mountain and watched the sunset together. I found my acquaintances at the harbor, walking around the polluted soil. They were astonished to see me. In the evening, upon returning to the hotel, I found out that the top minister of the Socialist government had arrived in town. "Now you'll see who you've been mimicking all this time," I told Aliki. Aliki was also the name of the minister's wife.

Next day, on the road to Kalamata, after Tripoli, the bear kept asking to be let out. I let it drag me, for the first time, like a dog following a scent. It took me to its old haunts. To its lair. It wanted to live there. I let it. Until one day, when it is found by a topographer who takes it home to his daughter Aliki who's involved with a young Gypsy; the Gypsy tells his father about the bear, and the story starts over. But where do I fit into this story? I am waiting for a phone call from my own Aliki. And while I'm waiting, I'm writing. And so on and so forth.

6. CONCLUSION, OR NARRATIVE ENDING

For the informed reader, I must say that there is no relation between my bear story and the poem "The Sacred Road" by Angelos Sikelianos. I don't have it with me at the moment, but I remember that in his poem about a bear (a species faced, sadly, with extinction, like the spinning wheel), the poet of "The Lyric Life" gives symbolic extensions. For Sikelianos, the bear symbolizes the history of a people (the Greek people, of course) bound with the chains of slavery and not wanting to dance to the beat of the tambourine played by its master; but in my case there is no symbolism. There is no hidden meaning to my story. It was simply my need to describe Athens during the holidays—

that reflection of misery and horror—that gave birth, in the little room of my mind, to the white bear, whose wandering around this sad setting amused me because it gave it a different touch. In front of the piles of clothes on Athinas Street; and in a shop on a small street behind the National Theater, which sells herbal teas, salep, and aromatic herbs from Chios, with an old publicity poster in English for the island's mastic, dating back fifty years, when there were neither any telexes nor any automatic telephones, and when going to America was not simply a matter of hours and when the Chiotes who had emigrated to the United States would sell the products of their native island in their new home; in front of a *Politis* (the journal), which reminds me of a woman without a lover becoming hysterical; an *Anti* (the magazine), which also reminds me of a woman, but one who sleeps with a different man each time without enjoying it; a *Commentator,* who seems to be taking pleasure in himself; and a *Reader,* which is a Lothario preying on foreign tourists. That is to say, full of translated texts, amid the vomitous daily press, I suffer the same kind of depression as in the center of Athens, and I search my brain for white bears that will enrich me with their presence in this downtown civilization that reproduces the cultural Kalamata (four *a*'s in a row: Kavála has but three; Patras, two; and Tziá, only one).

Translated by Mary Kitroëff

The Fresco

Marios Hakkas

IN THE MONASTERY at Kaisariani there exists a fresco in three panels, *The Victim of Robbers,* which does not wander far from the well-known description of the Gospel: a traveler falls into the hands of robbers; there follows the usual beating; the fine fellows leave having fallen in line, their cudgels on their shoulders as if they were soldiers; some passerby assists the victim.

At first glance the thing one notices is the inferiority of this mural, which perhaps creates a new aesthetic, as do all vulgar things one sees at first glance, and which naturally does not interest me in that sense. The thing that grabs me is that, because of this supposedly slipshod piece of work, a different meaning arises beyond the original parable, which coincides with several incidents that happened in the neighborhood of Kaisariani.

There is that similarity of the features—traveler, robbers, passerby—the same faces. I'm not talking about the uncovered parts of the body, otherwise few, and the pleated robes, completely the same, all of them, as if the iconographer had but one model in front of him. The faces, the faces, "victim" and "nonvictim," each the same. If he had put a contortion on the faces of the robbers as they lift their cudgels and strike the fallen traveler, or if he had drawn an expression of pain on the latter, the similarity between fresco and modern Kaisariani would have been ruined.

The basic inference is that the same person beats, is beaten, and rescues.

Now I understand why Honis, otherwise known as "Momma my doughnut," shouts slogans, works the megaphone, later becomes a member of the "H's" (a right-wing paramilitary organization), and in his turn beats up those who shout slogans, work the megaphone, and who earlier beat up "Momma my doughnut" because he shouted slogans and worked the megaphone. The same people, the same faces, one and only one model.

This also explains "Rouhou Mouhou," laundrynapper and police informer, who upon leaving Davila's house, where he had squealed, grabs the laundry—later he is nabbed in a dragnet and soundly thrashed; he continues, however, to take his information to Davila, but upon leaving the house no longer finds the laundry to steal, because Davila's wife, having foreseen his act, has hidden it.

"We all boil in the same pot," says an old man from the community, and I have no great objection as I study the fresco, if naturally we exclude the dead. They are outside of the game now, outside of every game. Only I don't know how long that pot will boil and what kind of sauce it will make in the end. I'm afraid that whatever sauce it was going to give has already been given, either because the pot had a hole in it, or else because it's no longer boiling. The people fade, new situations arise and overturn the old ones; the radio, the television, the electric bill, the phone bill. Nicknames are slowly disappearing. Apartment buildings are sprouting up on the boulevard, and the side streets are paved over.

I suspect that the old meaning of the fresco has become obsolete, and it seems to express something more current, that languid and homogenous something of consumer society, something general that is spreading—a monster—throughout all of Athens.

Kaisariani of credit at the grocer's, of brilliantine in the hair, you are finally dead. Kaisariani of Moukoutsou the shit-eater (I saw him eating his own excrement on a bet for an occupation-time hundred-drachma note leaning against the curb of the soccer field) he, that thereafter stool-pigeon and terrorist—and he even worked for both sides. Primeval Kaisariani, you no longer exist.

However, for me, my mind and my love is for the Kaisariani of "beatings," and it is a blessing that I lived and grew up there. Everything was wild and virginal, in its first incarnation, like the events of an ancient tragedy. Jason cut down the first tree he came across, made a ship, and raised sail for Colchis. Oedipus, tangled on the verge, blinds himself in the warm brightness of dawn. And Creon appears for the first time in the story with a large set of keys. All of them at the wellspring, at their first revelation, this is why people, neighborhoods, and events cannot be extinguished from within me.

A place that was inhabited for the first time. A long, narrow lane with tight curves. On the left, the stream and a forest—gaunt, sickly pines. On the right, the wall of the *Skopeftirio,* the Firing Range. High up, the monastery.

Tents, shanties, cinder-block hovels, the patchwork of the refugees, and there Kaisariani like a smile in the first light of dawn.

Kaisariani of the public rest rooms, of the milkman who spread propaganda for Russia and who was seized by the *Vourliotes* (another right-wing paramilitary organization) with billy clubs. Kaisariani of the pig headed, cudgel bearing, of "asphodel meatballs," I thank you that I was raised in your back alleys. What could one say and what could one admit who lived in Mesolongi? That past and that myth would bear down on him. Even as he approached, everything was gone for him, even the deterioration of the place was completed before his time.

Kaisariani, I thank you that I was fortunate to see and touch several people who left us at the right time, before they managed to associate themselves with whichever meaning of the fresco, whether "beating" or "consuming." For Lefteri, the brother of Mrs. Vdthokia—"Aslan Lefteri, Cap'n Lefteri"—who was later executed on Corfu. For Poutsouri, with whom I played with wooden swords and paper hats; later he held a carbine in his hand, a fifteen-year-old kid when a bullet found him at the front near Poseidona. Thank you that I deigned to see Apollo's blue jacket, more blue than ever I saw, from pure sky and sea. And Aris, killed on the corner of Damareos and Formionos; in that very spot I saw the corpses of several collaborators who hid their identity cards in their socks. A just and quick retribution, an automatic cleansing of the place.

Whom shall I first commemorate for you, Kaisariani? Ignatius who became reckless? He was the fool of the neighborhood and had been swept up by the general climate. In his back pocket he would put a clog—supposedly a revolver—and wander patrolling the neighborhoods, all precaution and great care. Somewhere they caught him in this suspicious stance, fired, and there he went.

Once, Kaisariani, you were a star, you shone for a moment in the firmament and were lost forever in the chaos of history.

Now, old Madam, you eat *sámali* and *touloumba*,* you chew sunflower seeds in the summertime open-air cinema, and you spit the husks on the backs of the necks of respectable merchants, businessman-grocers, butchers, contractors, who want to be exempt from your shame. From one point of view I agree with the mayor, who wants to change your name. What do you have to do with these small persons, with the spirit of ownership and exchange? They will call you New Vryoula or New Symvrisarion. Maybe they should. What remains of the district of St. Antoine in Paris except just the name? Its undulating parallel steppes have been irrigated, they're building in Kantona, Kokkinia became "*Nice*," the most worthy of your children were cut down. That's how it always happens after a wild felling of trees, and the few trees that remain are sickly. Let me not now make an appeal, "living and dead ... whose Kingdom shall have no end." It is the end of the season and the sales are to follow.

Kaisariani, I'm sweating. Kaisariani, I'm choking. Kaisariani, I'm nauseous. You sit at dusk and take your refreshment on the sidewalks, while your girls come down, purse

---

* *Sámali* is a kind of sweet made from farina, syrup, and eggs; *touloumba* is an oblong syrup-soaked cake.

in hand, for the market. You drink your orgeat with the money from brokers' fees and you burp. I grasp in your glance a remorse, as if you regret that from your birth you weren't a middleman, a pimp, and a collaborator.

Where is your spirit and where your freedom, gazelle, buck, and deer? Where is your beauty and your jewelry, frigate, schooner, and corvette?

Nothing remains. Now you plaster the final signs of machine-gun fire on your forehead, like an old dog licking its wounds to heal them. Now, downtrodden, crushed, overwhelmed, in the last panel of the fresco: refuge—and forgetfulness of the wild events of your journey.

Translation by Gerasimus Katsan

Funerary Epigrams

Odysseus Elytis

NO CLOUDS APPEAR on the horizon of Greek death. An openness always allows us to look at the inside of a house where life stopped and, at the proper moment, through some crack see the small patch of blue that was Plato's immortality. Always within the same terrifying calmness as that which follows a lightning strike. And not just anywhere, but against a rock. Where the absent one is kept solemn company by those present. As if they want to show how difficult it is to traverse *from both sides* the insignificant distance that divides one moment from the next—I mean the moment following death, the one that transforms the order of the world.

It is there for one to see: the impact the loss of human life can have. In Tragedy we see one extreme, in philosophical thought another; but in the world of the Greeks these very things are turned upside down before the spectacle of the Kerameikos cemetery. Here a feeling hovers, arrested in time, which is neither certainty for the expected nor uncertainty for the loss; a mere echo that before it is manifest cancels itself out, leaving you listening to two things at once, together and separately. This: "We all equally travel to the same false shore"; and this: "gathering the sacred flowers of good living," so that I may use the words of one and the same poet. Something that has lived on in the demotic songs of the Greek peoples down to our own day, without any form of Christian disapproval being able to alter it. Good thing, too. Since, after Christ's teaching of humility, everything points to our having become more hardened and far more self-centered. We take community to be a simple means to promote ourselves. We reject our personal life so that we may more easily become humans fit for some paradise or other. What medieval duke or what oil magnate of today could ever imagine it possible to be made everlasting together with his maidservant? Poor Mnesarete of Kerameikos! Your look, full of forgiveness, surpasses in power the sign of the cross, and it blesses whatever we call "priceless"—wherever it may be found.

The way in which a whole community understands life becomes imprinted through the way it makes use of matter. I mean to say, how this whole molds the material world to the needs of everyday life. Things in excess, the unjustified ornament, the wry grimace, all these spell for the Greek to this day a kind of "hubris," something one would never think of committing at so sacred a moment as the leap across the unknown. Whoever understands meaning as the thing it is, a sort of anthropomorphic reality, not only avoids giving shape to death (as the shape given those freakish skeletal remains with the seal on their cranium that we sophistically thought up in the early centuries of European civilization), but takes care to stand apart from whatever may smack of using one's pain and loss: an exaggeration, the breakdown in expression, the unchecked gesture, all the things which the European tradition later nurtured under a variety of guises of one and the same expressionism.

That the aesthetic lies in wait and conquers the ethical, up to a point, is nowhere as easily "readable" as on these commemorative *steles,* these tombstones. An arrangement of forms, an economy, the pleasing alignment, down to the most insignificant folds of a chiton, all point to a personal drama that agrees with the ethics a culture has developed based, above all, on dignity and self-respect. Here we begin to understand that all the weight falls on our shoulders, that no sooner does fear take two steps backward in our souls than hope takes two steps forward—just so we will not lose our balance; moments of sweetness are at once mobilized to even out those moments of bitterness; and that which is solemnized on approval, under the threat of heresy, continues to this day and must continue. Outrunning fate, humans ask to create another, a personal one tailored to size; and end up with empty hands, surprised before our frailty.

Freilich ist es seltsam, die Erde nicht mehr zu bewohnen, "Indeed it is strange not to dwell on earth anymore," so it fell to the poet of death to say twenty centuries later. The frieze in its essence—already halfway toward painting— expresses just this bewilderment. It allows us to trace the psychic fluctuations, without the danger of turning them into some anecdotal phase of our lives. A small wrinkle of a personal life, precisely because it has no meaning for others, acquires the power of uniqueness and becomes a detail in the artist's depiction.

It is never night or morning, since time has no longer any meaning. But it is always the home, the family, the loved ones, the thread we held onto that keeps unwinding directly from our heart. That girl who looks out with resignation; and the other one opening the jewel box; and the one who prepares to offer the mirror but hesitates, as if she sensed the uselessness of it; or the old man who had thought he first would touch the future moment, but—the little boy is there and looks about to fall asleep—what of all that would be altered now?—and the dog that smells the edge of the cloth. You would say, just letters all of them, letters of an artist's alphabet, if nothing else, that give us the opportunity to sketch out a depiction of our thirst for eternity in the most discreet manner.

TIMARISTOS AND KRITO, KTESILEOS AND THEANO. HEGESO, AMYNOKLEIA, MNESARETE, MYNNO—how puzzling! These capital letters in stone, nothing else mentioned, no further comment; these trace us back and locate us. They create the calm of a shadow within the blinding light of death. We walk in a garden perfect as a clock whose hands are gone, where the tightening of the heart always points to noon. A *kore*, so young, so beautiful—it's not possible—surely she's still somewhere combing away at her hair; that's why the air is fragrant and the sheets in disarray when we awaken.

Somewhere a cicada falls silent at three in the afternoon. Then all the rest are quiet too. The cloud passes over. The great events of our lives are those we let slip through our fingers, so that we may hold onto crusades and heroes— what an affliction! If there is a side to human sensitivity that goes without notice, it is exactly that affliction. That side drives us to the other extreme where all the noise is, where one day, surprised, we see it passing from the province of the poet to the authority of the marble craftsman, never losing anything of its transcendent nature.

The known fact: no great sculptor took on *funerary steles,* so that most of these, if not all, are the product of simple craftsmen who were left without a job after the completion of work on the Acropolis. This fact, rather than diminishing the *steles,* makes them even more meaningful. It bears witness to the benefit these men gained from Phidias's example, while at the same time as craftsmen they dwelled so near a widely cultivated community. Nobility, when it becomes common domain, multiplies in size. Then it seeks to be reduced to its elementary form.

It is true that, from such a viewpoint, each *stele* strives for a monumental architectonic through the least possible means. The ever changing dimensions, along with the ever different and necessary decorative elements, provided a large enough variety (one has only to consider the *steles* of Salamina, of Hegeso, or of Giustiniani) and a symmetrical proportion, which, for as long as a give-and-take among the various parts of our soul had not been settled, fully complemented the higher meaning of our lives.

The stone offered to Death as matter reconciles us with the tangible and the imperishable, and also submits itself to this higher meaning. We today look expectantly toward a symbol and turn to the cross; and in compliance with our repeating it exactly, we have transformed each necropolis into a rectilinear alignment in military fashion; the Greeks, more realistic, said "yes" to life, acquiesced in the essential and were satisfied with that. And it is that which has taken them to the heavens. A heaven full of rocks and pine trees and red earth. Where burnt laurel raises its smoke, and late afternoon becomes rose and violet, with a second Hymettos in the distance.

Ti odo cantare como una cicala
Nella rosa abbrunata dei riflessi . . .

Translation by John Chioles

Pilgrimage Through Greece

Nikos Kazantzakis

MY FATHER had promised me a year of travel, wherever I wanted to go, if I took my degree with highest honors. The reward was a great one, and I threw myself heart and soul into my studies. One of my friends, a devilishly clever Cretan, was going to take his examinations with me. The crucial day arrived. We started together for the university, both extremely uneasy. I had known everything and forgotten everything. My memory was a void; I felt terrified.

"Do you remember anything at all?" my friend asked me.

"Not a thing."

"Neither do I. Let's go to a beerhall to drink, get soused, and loosen our tongues. That's the way my father went to war—drunk."

"Come on."

We drank, drank some more, began to feel happy.

"How does the world look to you?" asked my friend.

"Double."

"Me too. Can you walk?"

I got up and took a few steps.

"Yes," I answered.

"Then let's go. Roman Law—tremble!"

We set out arm in arm at first, but then each worked up courage and continued on his own two feet.

"Hi, Bacchus my stalwart!" I cried. "Give Justinian and his Novels the old hammer lock. Lay him out cold on the ground!"

"Why call on Bacchus?" my friend asked. "We drank beer, not wine."

"Are you sure?"

"You don't believe me? Let's go back and ask."

We went back.

"Beer, beer," the owner of the establishment assured us, splitting his sides with laughter. "Where are you headed, gents?"

"To take our law exams."

"Wait, I'll come along for the laughs."

He removed his apron and followed behind. The professors were waiting for us. Enthroned as they were, all in a row, they seemed like so many gnats. Our brains spat fire. With immense gusto we answered their questions, answered them with a nonchalance somewhat insolent, mixing in Latin tags with great frequency. Our tongues wagged incessantly, and we both came out with highest honors.

We were overjoyed. My friend planned to establish a law office in Crete and enter politics, while I rejoiced because a door of escape was opening for me. All my life one of my greatest desires has been to travel—to see and touch unknown countries, to swim in unknown seas, to circle the globe, observing new lands, seas, peoples, and ideas with insatiable appetite, to see everything for the first time and for the last time, casting a slow, prolonged glance, then to close my eyes and feel the riches deposit themselves inside me calmly or stormily according to their pleasure, until time passes them at last through its fine sieve, straining the quintessence out of all the joys and sorrows. This alchemy of the heart is, I believe, a great delight which all men deserve.

The canary, the magic bird my father gave me as a New Year's present when I was a child, had become a carcass years before; no, not "become a carcass"—I blush that this expression escaped me—had "passed away" I meant to say, passed away like a human. Or better still, had "rendered its song up to God." We buried it in our little courtyard-garden. My sister cried, but I was calm because I knew that as long as I remained alive, I would never allow it to perish. "I won't let you perish," I whispered as I covered it over with earth. "We shall live and travel together."

When I grew older, left Crete, and wandered over the earth's surface, I always felt this canary clinging to my scalp and singing—singing the identical refrain over and over again, incessantly: "Let's get up and leave. Why are we sitting here? We are birds, not oysters. Let's get up and leave." My head had become a terrestrial globe with the canary, perched at its pole, raising its warm throat toward heaven and singing.

I've heard that in the old days the concubines of the harem stood in a row each evening in their garden, freshly bathed and scented, their breasts uncovered, and the sultan came down to make his choice. In his hand he held a little handkerchief which he thrust beneath the armpit of each and then sniffed. He chose the woman whose aroma pleased him the most that evening.

It was like concubines that the various countries lined themselves up in a row before me.

Hastily, avidly, I swept my eyes over the map. Where to go? Which continent, which ocean to see first? All the countries held out their hands and invited me. The world was extensive, praise the Lord, and—let idlers say what they will—man's life was extensive too. We would have time to see and enjoy all countries.

Why not begin with Greece!

My pilgrimage through Greece lasted three months. Even now after so many years my heart throbs with happiness and inquietude when I recall the mountains, islands, villages, monasteries, and coastlines. It is a great joy to travel through Greece and see it, a great joy and an agony.

I traveled through Greece, and gradually I began to see with my eyes and touch with my hands something that abstract thought cannot touch or see: the means by which strength and grace combine. I doubt that these two ingredients of perfection, Ares and Aphrodite, have ever joined together so organically in any other part of the world, have ever joined together so organically as in the austere, ever-smiling land of Greece. Some of her regions are severe and haughty, others full of feminine tenderness, still others serious and at the same time cheerful and gracious. But the spirit passed over all of them and by means of a temple, myth, or hero bequeathed the proper, suitable soul to each. That is why whoever journeys in Greece and has eyes to see with and a mind to think with, journeys in an unbroken magical unity from one spiritual victory to another. In

Greece a person confirms the fact that spirit is the continuation and flower of matter, and myth the simple, composite expression of the most positive reality. The spirit has trodden upon the stones of Greece for many, many years; no matter where you go, you discover its divine traces.

Various regions in Greece are dual in nature, and the emotion that springs from them is also dual in nature. Harshness and tenderness stand side by side, complementing each other and coupling like a man with a woman. Sparta is one such source of tenderness and harshness. In front of you stands Taygetus, a hard, disdainful legislator full of cliffs and precipices, while below, stretched out at your feet like a woman in love, is the fruited, seductive plain. On the one hand Taygetus, the Mount Sinai of Greece, where the pitiless god of the Race dictates the most rigid of commandments: life is war, the world is a battlefield, your sole duty is to win; do not sleep, do not adorn yourselves, laugh, or talk; fighting is your sole purpose in life, therefore fight! And on the other hand, at Taygetus's foot—Helen. Just as you begin to grow savage and to disdain the earth's sweetness, suddenly Helen's breath, like a flowering lemon tree, makes your mind reel.

Is this Spartan plain really so tender and voluptuous? I wonder. Is the fragrance of its oleanders really so intoxicating—or does all this fascination perhaps spring from Helen's oft-kissed far-roving body? Certainly Eurotas would not possess its present-day seductive grace had it not flowed as a tributary into Helen's immortal myth. For lands, seas, and rivers, as we well know, join with great beloved names and, evermore inseparable from them, flow into our hearts. Walk along the humble banks of the Eurotas and you feel your hands, hair, and thoughts become entangled in the perfume of an imaginary woman far more real, far more tangible, than the woman you love and touch. The world today is drowning in blood, passions rage in our present-day anarchistic hell, yet Helen, immortal and untouched, stands unmovable in the air of her extraordinary verses while time flows by in front of her.

The soil was fragrant; the dewdrops hanging from the lemon flowers capered in the sunlight. Suddenly a gentle breeze blew and a flower struck my forehead, sprinkling me with dew. A quiver ran through me, as though I had been touched by an invisible hand. The whole earth seemed a freshly bathed, laughing-weeping Helen. She was lifting her veils with their embroidered lemon flowers and, her palm to her mouth, her virginity constantly renewed, following a man, the strongest that could be found. And as she raised her legs with their snow-white ankles, the round soles of her feet gleamed with blood.

What would this Helen have been if Homer's breath had not passed over her? A beautiful woman like countless others who made their passage across this earth and perished. She would have been abducted, just as pretty girls are still frequently abducted in our mountain villages. And even if this abduction had ignited a war, everything—the war, the woman, the slaughter—would have perished if the Poet had not reached out his hand to save them. It is to the Poet that Helen owes her salvation; it is to Homer that this tiny riverbed, Eurotas, owes its immortality. Helen's smile suffuses all the Spartan air. But even beyond this, she has entered our very bloodstreams. Every man has partaken of her in communion; to this day every woman reflects her splendor. Helen has become a love cry. She traverses the centuries, awakens in every man the yearning for kisses and perpetuation. She transforms every woman we clasp to our breast, even the most commonplace, into a Helen.

Thanks to this Spartan queen, sexual desire assumes exalted titles of nobility; the secret nostalgia for some lost embrace sweetens the brute within us. When we weep or cry out, Helen throws a magic herb into the bitter dram we are drinking, and we completely forget our pain. In her hand she holds a flower whose scent drives off serpents. At her touch ugly children become beautiful. She straddles the goat of the ancient Bacchic rites, shakes her foot with its untied sandal, and the entire world is transformed into a vineyard. One day when the ancient poet Stesichorus uttered an uncomplimentary word about her in one of his odes, he was immediately struck blind. Then, trembling and repentant, he took his lyre, stood up before the Greeks at a great festival, and sang the famous palinode:

> *What I said about you is not true, Helen;*
> *you never boarded the swift ships,*
> *nor did you ever reach the citadel of Troy.*

He wept, holding his hands aloft; and all at once the light, submerged in tears, descended to the corners of his eyes.

Our ancestors held beauty contests in her honor, the "Heleneia." Truly, the earth is a palaestra and Helen the unattainable achievement, the achievement beyond life, perhaps nonexistent, perhaps just a phantom. In one of the mystery cults the tradition confided to initiates was that the Achaeans did not fight at Troy for the true Helen, that only her image was discovered in Troy, that the real Helen had found refuge in Egypt, in a sacred temple where she remained untouched by human breath. Who knows—perhaps we too fight, weep, and kill each other here on earth only for Helen's image. But on the other hand, who knows (the shades in Hades came to life when they drank the blood of a living man)—with all the blood that Helen's shade has drunk over so many thousands of years, will it never be able to come to life again? I wonder. I wonder if the image will not eventually join its flesh, thus enabling us one day to embrace a real, warm body, a true Helen?

Taygetus the fierce warrior and Helen his wife. Inhaling Helen's perfume amid the oleanders of the Eurotas, I had forgotten myself. I felt ashamed. In order to breathe more virile air I set out one morning to climb Taygetus.

The mountain's cheer, the pine tree's balm, the fiery rocks, the hawks hovering above me, the impregnable solitude—all these fortified my heart. I climbed happily for many hours. Around noontime, however, black clouds gathered overhead. There were muffled thunderclaps. I started back down at a run, feeling the storm approaching behind me. I jumped from stone to stone, raced, competed with it so that it would not overtake me. But suddenly the pines quivered, the world grew dark, and I was belted by lightning flashes. The whirlwind had caught me. Plunging face downward on the ground so that I would not fall, I closed my eyes and waited. The whole mountain shook; next to me two pines split in half and thundered down the slope. I smelled the sulphur in the air. All at once the torrent let loose. The wind subsided and huge necklaces of water poured out of the sky. The thyme, savory, sage, and mint, battered by the downpour, threw forth their scents; the entire mountain began to steam.

Getting up, I resumed the descent, rejoicing to have the water thrash my face, hair, and hands. Zeus the Descender was falling with all his might upon Earth, his suffocating wife, who split open with cackling laughter and received the male waters.

Soon the sky cleared. The storm had been a violent descent of the Holy Ghost; now, as the cuckoo began to proclaim, it was finished. At that very moment the sun went down. Far in the distance below me I spied the freshly bathed ruins of the Frankish citadel of the Villehardouins at the top of its hill, above Mistra. The entire sky had turned gold and green.

The next day, proceeding through orchards and cypress groves, I went as a pilgrim to Mistra, the Greek Pompeii. This sacred hill, the birthplace of modern Greece, possesses all the manifest and hidden charms needed to entice even the most difficult of souls: lemon and orange trees, narrow twisting lanes, half-naked children playing in the streets, women going for water, girls sitting beneath blossoming trees and embroidering. Life has begun to cling to this soil again; it is struggling to reclimb the whole of the ancestral hill. This is Mistra's first zone, the green and inhabited one. Proceed farther and the dusty, treeless ascent begins. Striding through crumbled houses, you reach the charming sunbaked Byzantine churches—Perívleptos, Metrópoli, Aghioi Theodoroi, Aphendikó, Pandánassa. This is Mistra's second zone, and it is studded with churches.

I was thirsty. I entered the Pandánassa convent to have

the nuns offer me a glass of water. The courtyard was shining, the cells whitewashed and immaculate, the sofas covered with embroidered woolen blankets. The nuns ran to welcome me. Some were young, others stiff from rheumatism, all inordinately pale because they must work very hard in order to subsist. They keep vigils, they pray, and they never have enough food to calm their hunger. When they have a free hour, they bend over their handwork and embroider traditional motifs—tiny roses out of red silk thread, crosses, monasteries, vases full of carnations, little cypress trees. You are overcome with sadness when they proudly spread these embroideries before you, as though showing you their dowries. They smile, say nothing, but you know that the bridegroom does not exist.

Pandánassa gleamed in the honey-green twilight like a small Byzantine pyx of ivory, worked with patience and love to house the Virgin's sweetly effluent breath. What unity, concentration, and grace this church possesses, from the cornerstone of the foundation to the erotic curves of the dome! The whole of the charming temple lives and breathes, peacefully, like a warm animate organism. All the stones, carvings, paintings, and nuns exist as organic ingredients of this convent, as though one midday they had all been born simultaneously, from the same procreative shudder.

I had never expected to find such tenderness and warm human understanding in Byzantine paintings. Previous to this I had seen only fierce ascetic forms holding parchments covered with red letters and calling to us to despise nature and flee to the desert; to die in order to be saved. But now here were splendid colors, here were faces of the utmost sweetness. Christ entering Jerusalem on his humble beast, kindly and smiling, the disciples following with palm branches, and the populace gazing at them with ecstatic eyes, as at a cloud which passes and then scatters. . . . And the angel I saw at Aphendikó, a beautiful stalwart the green color of oxidized brass, his curly hair bound in a wide ribbon. With his impulsive stride and firm round knees he resembled a bridegroom heading for— But where was he heading with such joy and haste?

Just at that moment the bell began to ring softly, sweetly, for the Good Friday vigil. I entered the church's warm, domed interior. In the center, covered with lemon flowers, was the *epitáphios,* the sepulchral canopy, and lying dead upon the lemon flowers, He who is incessantly dying, incessantly resurrected. Once He was called Adonis, now Christ. Pale black-robed women were kneeling around Him, bending over Him, bewailing Him. The entire church smelled of wax, like a beehive. I thought of those other priestesses, the Melissae, at the temple of the Ephesian Artemis; also the temple of Apollo at Delphi, built of wax and feathers.

Suddenly the women's laments, the unbearable dirge, broke out in full force. I knew that human suffering was the force that would resurrect God, but here in Helen's kingdom my heart was not at all prepared to wail. Darkness had not fallen yet; I rose and continued to climb this hill with its ruined mansions, its towers sprawled on the ground, and, like a stone crown at the summit, the celebrated citadel of the Villehardouins. The great fortified gate was open, the courtyards deserted. I mounted the crumbling stairs and reached the battlements, forcing a surprised flock of crows to take wing. I looked down at the fertile plain below me and at the smoke that rose from the squat cottages; I could hear the creaking of a cart and a song filled with passion. The atmosphere all around me heaved a sigh. Specters filled the air. The blond daughters of Frankish seigneurs rose from the grave, together with the armor-encased knights who came here to the Peloponnesus in the role of conquerors, married Greek girls, became inoculated with Greek blood, and forgot their homeland. Thanks to our dark-skinned women with their raven-black hair and large eyes, the victors were vanquished.

A few days later I enjoyed another scene. You cross a dry riverbed shaded by plane trees and beflowered by osiers, you climb an austere mountain fragrant with savory and thyme, devoid of villages, people, goats, and sheep—utterly forsaken. Then, suddenly, behind a turn in the terrain, looming unexpectedly before you in the heart of the Peloponnesus is the famous temple of Apollo at Bassae. It is constructed from the same gray stones that compose the mountain, and the moment you face it, you sense the profound correspondence between temple and site. It seems a piece of the mountain, rock of its rock, wedged indistinguishably between the crags—itself a crag, but one over which the spirit has passed. Carved and placed as they are, the columns of this temple express the very essence of all this montigenous austerity and forsakenness. It is as though the temple were the cranium of the surrounding landscape, the sacred mound-circle inside whose sheltered precincts the mind of the site keeps ever-vigilant watch. Here the artistry of the ancients, continuing and expressing the landscape to perfection, does not make you gasp with astonishment. It lifts you to the summit along a human pathway, so gently and dexterously that you do not grow short of breath. You might say that the entire mountain had been longing for eons inside its tenebrous bulk to find expression, and that the moment it acquired this temple of Apollo, it felt relieved. Felt relieved—in other words, assumed a meaning, its own meaning, and rejoiced.

Each day as I walked over the Greek land, I realized more clearly that ancient Greek civilization was not a supernatural flower suspended in midair; it was a tree that rooted itself deeply in the earth, consumed mud, and turned this mud into flowers. And the more mud it consumed, the more richly elaborate did this flowering become. The ancients' splendid simplicity, balance, and serenity were not the natural, easily achieved virtues of a simple and balanced race. They were difficult exploits, the spoils of painful, dangerous campaigns. Greek serenity is intricate and tragic, a balance between fierce opposing forces that after a toilsome and prolonged struggle succeeded in making peace with one another and in reaching the point prescribed by a Byzantine mystic—effortlessness. In other words, effort's peak.

The factor that renders Greece's mountains, villages, and soil buoyant and immaterial is the light. In Italy the light is soft and feminine, in Ionia extremely gentle and full of oriental yearning, in Egypt thick and voluptuous. In Greece the light is entirely spiritual. Able to see clearly in this light, man succeeded in imposing order over chaos, in establishing a "cosmos"—and cosmos means harmony.

A little old lady emerged from the custodian's hut next

to the temple. She held two figs and a bunch of grapes in her palm. They were the first to ripen on this high plateau, and she wished to present them to me as a gift. She was a sweet, thin, jovial old lady who surely must have beamed with radiance in her youth.

"What's your name?" I asked her.

"Maria."

But as she saw me grasp a pencil to make note of this name, she extended her wrinkled hand to stop me.

"Mariyítsa," she said with juvenile coquetry. "Mariyítsa."

Since her name was to be perpetuated in writing, she seemed to want to save her other name, the pet one. This would awaken life's sweetest moments in her memory.

"Mariyítsa . . . ," she repeated, as though afraid I had failed to hear.

I was glad to see the eternal feminine rooted even in this most ramshackle of bodies.

"What's all this around us?" I asked her.

"Don't you see? Stones."

"And why do people come from the ends of the earth to see them?"

The old woman hesitated a moment. Then, lowering her voice, she asked me, "Are you a foreigner?"

"No, Greek."

Encouraged, she shrugged her shoulders.

"Foreign idiots!" she exclaimed, bursting into laughter.

This was not the first time I saw these old ladies, the ones who watch over ancient temples or famous churches containing wonder-working icons, laugh sacrilegiously at the saints or ancient marble demons they guard. They associate with them daily, after all, and familiarity breeds contempt.

Old Mariyítsa watched me with satisfaction as I pecked at the pleasantly tart grapes she had given me.

"And what do you think about politics?" I asked, trying to tease her.

"Eh! my boy," she answered with unexpected pride, "we're very high up here, removed from the world, and we don't hear its racket."

We—in other words, "the temple and myself." And she had uttered the word *removed* in a proud tone that meant *superior*. I felt glad. The old woman's remark, even more than the temple itself, satisfied my heart to the full.

I walked to and fro beneath the columns. It had rained two days before, and pools of water still lay motionless and clear in the hollows of the broken marble. Leaning over, I saw fluffy white clouds pass like ghosts across the water's surface. I had read that divinity had once been worshiped similarly in the Far East, in water-filled hollows over which clouds passed.

As I was returning to the plain, I saw an old man kneeling on the stones. He was leaning over a channel and watching the water run, his face bathed in inexpressible ecstasy. It seemed as though his nose, mouth, and cheeks had vanished; nothing remained but the two eyes that followed the water as it flowed between the rocks. I went up to him.

"What do you see there, old man?" I asked him.

And he, without lifting his head or removing his eyes from the water, replied, "My life, my life which is running out . . ."

All things in Greece—mountains, rivers, seas, valleys—become "humanized": they speak to man in a language that is almost human. They do not torment or crushingly over-whelm him; they become his friends and fellow workers. The turbid, unsettled cry of the Orient grows pellucid when it passes through the light of Greece; humanized, it is trans-formed into *logos*—reason. Greece is the filter that, with great struggle, refines brute into man, eastern servitude into liberty, barbaric intoxication into sober rationality. To give features to the featureless and measure to the measureless, balancing the blind clashing forces—such is the mission of the much-buffeted sea and land known as Greece.

To travel through Greece is a true joy, a great enrichment. The Greek soil has been so saturated with blood, sweat, and tears, the Greek mountains have witnessed so much human struggle, that you shudder in contemplating the fact that here, on these mountains and shores, the destiny of the white race—of all mankind—was at stake. Surely it must have been on one of these shores so filled with grace and frolicsomeness that the miraculous transformation of beast into man took place. It must have been on such a Greek strand that Astarte of the multitudinous sowlike breasts cast anchor from Asia Minor, and the Greeks, receiving the barbaric and coarsely carved wooden statue, cleansed it of its bestiality, left it with only the two human breasts, and gave it a human body full of nobility. From Asia Minor the Greeks took primitive instinct, orgiastic intoxication, the bestial shout—Astarte. They transubstan-tiated the instinct into love, the bite into kisses, the orgy into religious worship, the shout into the lover's endear-ment. Astarte they transformed into Aphrodite.

Greece's spiritual as well as geographical location carries with it a mystic sense of mission and responsibility. Because two continually active currents collide on her land and seas, she has always been a place subjected both geographically and spiritually to incessant whirlpools. This fated location has exerted a fundamental influence on Greece's lot and also the lot of the entire world.

I viewed, smelled, and touched Greece, proceeding all alone on foot, an olivewood staff in my hand and a carpet-bag over my shoulder. And as Greece penetrated increasingly within me, I felt with ever-increasing depth that the mystic essence of her land and sea is musical. At every moment the Greek landscape changes slightly and yet remains the same; makes its beauty undulate, renews itself. It has a profound unity and at the same time a constantly renewed diversity. I wonder if this same rhythm did not govern the art of the ancient Greeks, an art that was born in regarding, loving, understanding, and giving concrete expression to the visible world around it. Look at a work of the great classical period. It is not motionless; an imperceptible quiver of life pervades it. Just as the hawk when it hesitates at the zenith of its flight—its wings beat, and yet to us it appears immobile—so in the same way the ancient statue moves imperceptibly and lives. In one immortal instant that both continues artistic tradition and makes ready art's future course, it holds the threefold flux of time in perfect equilibrium.

By means of their struggles the Greeks sanctified each region, subordinated each to an exalted meaning that formed its definitive essence. By means of beauty and disciplined passion they converted each region's physical nature into something metaphysical. Pushing aside grass, soil, and stones, they discovered the region's cool, cool soul

deep beneath the ground. This soul they embodied sometimes in a graceful temple, sometimes in a myth, and sometimes in a happy indigenous god.

For hours on end I gazed at Olympia's sacred landscape
—its nobility and meditative tranquillity, the cheerful, wel-
coming valley between domesticated foothills that screen
it from the fierce north wind, the scorching south wind,
and leave it exposed only on the western side toward the
water, whence arrives the cool sea breeze, ascending the
course of the Alpheus. No other site in Greece incites a
feeling of peace and concord in you so gently, so com-
pellingly. With unerring eyes the ancients designated it as
the place where all the Greek stocks would meet together
in brotherhood every four years, and in so designating it
they filled it with meaning and increased its tranquillity
and its power to instigate reconciliation.

Greece was torn by jealousies, hatreds, civil wars.
Democracies, aristocracies, and tyrannies exterminated one
another. The closed gorges, sequestered islands, secluded
coastlines, and small independent city-states created a single multiheaded organism rent by mutual hatred, and passions boiled in every breast. Then suddenly, every four
years, garlanded heralds, the *spondophoroi*, set out from this
sacred valley in summertime and ran to the farthest bound-
aries of the Greek world. They proclaimed the *hieromenia*,
the "sacred month" of the games, declared a general truce,
and invited friends and enemies alike to come to Olympia
in order to compete. From the whole of the Peloponnesus
and continental Greece, from Macedonia, Thessaly,
Epirus, and Thrace, from the shores of the Black Sea, Asia
Minor, Egypt, and Cyrene, from Magna Graecia and

Sicily, athletes and pilgrims sped to the sacred Panhellenic cradle of sport. Slaves were not allowed to set foot here, nor were criminals, foreigners, or women. Only free Greeks.

No other people had comprehended sport's hidden and manifest value so perfectly. When life has succeeded by dint of daily effort in conquering the enemies around it—natural forces, wild beasts, hunger, thirst, sickness—sometimes it is lucky enough to have abundant strength left over. This strength it seeks to squander in sport. Civilization begins at the moment sport begins. As long as life struggles for preservation—to protect itself from its enemies, maintain itself upon the surface of the earth—civilization cannot be born. It is born the moment that life satisfies its primary needs and begins to enjoy a little leisure.

How is this leisure to be used, how apportioned among the various social classes, how increased and refined to the utmost? According to how each race and epoch solves these problems, the worth and substance of its civilization can be judged.

I walked back and forth among the ruins of the Altis, joyfully viewing the shell-bearing stones employed to build the temples. These stones have been smashed by Christians and devastated by earthquakes. Rains and Alphean floods have washed away their stunning iridescence. The statues have been burned for lime; few remain to us, but these suffice to console our minds. I picked two or three sprigs of mint that had sprouted in the hollow where Phidias's gold and ivory statue is reputed to have stood, and the eternal scent filled my fingers.

Man wrestled in this mystic place, but the gods wrestled here before him. Zeus fought Chronos, his father, in order to take away his kingdom. Apollo, the god of light, defeated Hermes in running and Ares in boxing—mind conquered time, light conquered the dark forces of fraud and violence. Heroes were the next to contend here, after the gods. Pelops came from Asia, defeated the bloodthirsty barbarian Oenomaus and wedded his horse-taming daughter Hippodamia. The advanced Ionian civilization, so full of serenity and grace, defeated the unpolished natives of this region, brought the horse under subjection, and solidified man's might. Another hero, Heracles, having cleaned the Augean stables, came here to offer up great sacrifices to Zeus, the new god. With the ashes remaining from the victims he burned, he raised an altar and proclaimed the first Olympic games. This divine altar was raised continually higher with the ashes from new sacrifices, and Olympia became ever-increasingly the great workshop where the various Greek stocks forged their bronze bodies.

They did not do this simply to make these bodies beautiful. The Greeks never served art for its own sake. Beauty always had a purpose: to be of service to life. The ancients wanted their bodies strong and beautiful so that these bodies might be receptacles for balanced, healthy minds. And beyond this—the supreme purpose—so that they might defend the polis.

For the Greeks, gymnastics was a required preparation for each citizen's life as a member of society. The perfect citizen was the man who by frequenting the gymnasium and palaestra, was able to develop a body both strong and harmonious, in other words, beautiful, and have this body ready to defend the Race. Look at a statue from the classic age and you know at once whether the man portrayed was free or a slave. His body discloses it. A serene bearing, passion that is perfectly disciplined, a beautiful athletic form: these characterize the free man. The slave is always portrayed with abrupt unbridled gestures and a body either fat or sickly. Dionysus, the god of intoxication, stands calmly by while around him the besotted sileni and satyrs, his slaves and inferiors, behave indecently and perform their obscene dances.

Harmony of mind and body—that was the Greeks' supreme ideal. Hypertrophy of one to the detriment of the other they considered barbaric. When Greece began to decline, the athlete's body began at the same time to hypertrophy and to kill his mind. Euripides was among the first to protest; he proclaimed what risks the spirit was running at the hands of athleticism. Later, Galen added his denunciation: "They eat, drink, sleep, evacuate their bellies, and roll in dust and mud—behold what life the athletes lead." Heracles, the great martyr, who in the glorious years passed from exploit to exploit balancing mind and body to perfection, gradually degenerated into the huge-bodied, low-browed "wine-bibber and ox-eater." And the artists, who in the great eras had created the ideal type of the youthful form, now took to representing the athletic bodies they saw around them with raw realism, heavy and barbaric.

In Greece, as everywhere, once realism begins to reign, civilization declines. Thus we arrive at the realistic, magniloquent, and faithless Hellenistic era, which was devoid of suprapersonal ideals. From chaos to the Parthenon, then from the Parthenon back to chaos—the great merciless rhythm. Emotions and passions run wild. The free individual loses his powers of discipline; the bridle which maintained instinct in strict balance flies from his hands. Passion, emotionality, realism . . . A mystical, melancholy yearning suffuses the faces. The fearful mythological visions become merely decorative. Aphrodite undrapes herself like an ordinary woman, Zeus acquires roguishness and elegance, and Heracles regresses to a brute. After the Peloponnesian war Greece begins to disintegrate. Belief in the fatherland is lost; individual self-sufficiency triumphs. On the stage the protagonist is no longer God or the idealized youth, he is the wealthy citizen with his lascivious pleasures and passions—a materialist, skeptic, and libertine. Talent had already replaced genius; now good taste replaces talent. Art becomes filled with children, coquettish women, realistic scenes, and men either brutal or intellectual.

I climbed the hillock leading to the museum, hurrying to see Praxiteles' Hermes, the feats of Heracles, and the two marvelous pediments that have survived—hurrying, as though afraid that before I arrived the soil might have swallowed these remains as well. Why? Perhaps because man's lofty toil transgresses the inhuman laws of eternity. (Thus our life and our endeavors acquire a tragic, heroic intensity. We have but a single moment at our disposal. Let us transform that moment into eternity. No other form of immortality exists.)

My heart relaxed when I encountered the museum's great hall. Apollo, Heracles, Nike, the centaurs, and the Lapithae were all glowing peacefully in the morning light, all still alive. I rejoiced. This world of ours follows extrahuman laws. We sense, in these fatal times in which it is our lot to live, that at any moment a bomb might fall and reduce man's most precious memorials to ashes. When we greet a work of art now, our pleasure is tightly interwoven with the danger of everlasting separation which overhangs that work.

Looking at the two great pediments here, you realize how accurately a certain Far Eastern sage formulated the purpose of art when he said, "Art is the representation not of the body but of the forces that created the body." These creative forces rage visibly beneath the transparent surface here, especially in the western pediment. The banquet has just terminated; the intoxicated centaurs have charged in order to seize the women of the Lapithae. One of them sprints forward and embraces a woman, at the same time squeezing her breast with his huge hand. She seems to have swooned from the pain, and also from a mysterious, indescribable delight. Elsewhere the combatants bite and stab one another. The beast has been let loose in a savage outburst of violent passion; age-old scenes somewhere between man and ape-man are revived before our eyes. A mystic tranquillity, however, extends over all this astonishing primitive passion, because standing with perfect composure in the midst of the frenzied people, invisible to all the combatants, is Apollo, his right arm, and only his right arm, stretched out horizontally.

Though the sculptor who created this great scene, a few years before the Parthenon, had already surpassed the virgin awkwardness of the archaic artist, he still had not reached the artistic perfection of the classic moment. He was still in the midst of the assault, he had not touched the summit, and he was burning with a passionate, impatient desire to attain victory. He had smashed one equilibrium but had not reached the next; full of panting impetuosity, he was racing toward the final destination. If this pediment moves us so profoundly, it is because it still has not attained man's highest summit, the summit of perfection. One is still able to discern the suffering, struggling hero.

There is still another pleasure here. On this pediment you distinguish all the ranks of the hierarchy: god, free men, women, slaves, beasts. God stands in the middle, erect and calm, lord of his strength. Though he sees the horror around him, he is not disturbed. He controls his wrath and passion without, on the other hand, remaining indifferent, for he calmly extends his arm and grants the victory to the party he likes. The free men—the Lapithae—also maintain the human stamp on their faces, maintain it as immobile as they can. They do not howl, do not fall prey to panic. They are men, however, not gods, and a slight pulsation on their lips in addition to a wrinkle on the brow discloses that they are suffering. The women are suffering even more, but their pain merges unspeakably with a dark desire. In spite of themselves they seem glad to be seized by terrifyingly masculine brutes, glad to be shedding blood for their sakes. The slaves, on the other hand, are lounging about with presumptuous familiarity as they watch the others. They lack strict restraint. In the period when this pediment was created, these reclining forms at the edges could not represent gods. The gods would never have wallowed in such a way, never have forgotten their sacerdotal dignity. Finally, we have the centaurs, the debauched drunken beasts. Howling and biting, they pounce upon the women and boys. The mind is absent, and thus there is no force to impose order upon their strength or nobility upon their passion.

It is an extraordinary moment, this moment in which all the graduated ranks of life preserve their features intact. In this enmarbled moment all the elements coexist: the divine imperturbability, the free man's discipline, the beast's outburst, the realistic representation of the slave. A few generations afterward the latter two, the lowest elements, were to rule. Realistic passion would spread out and disfigure both the free man and the gods. The rein would be left slack, and art would bolt and decline. From the dynamic tragicality of this Olympic pediment and the divine calm of the Parthenon we would arrive at the unbridled verbalism of Pergamum.

On this pediment we have the pleasure of seeing all the seeds of acme, pro-acme, and post-acme coexisting in one conjoint flash. Perfection is a momentary equilibrium above chaos, a most difficult and dangerous balance. Throw a little weight to one side or the other, and it falls.

This pediment grants us still another pleasure. We look at it, and many questions arise. It came into being immediately after the Greek forces defeated the Persians and a happy wave of relief, pride, and strength poured over the entire land. Greece felt its might. The world around it and within it was renewed, gods and men were illuminated with a new light. Now everything else had to be renewed as well: temples, statues, paintings, poems. An everlasting memorial to the Greek victories over the barbarians had to be erected. What sculptural form was this memorial to take?

The great artist looks beneath the flux of everyday reality and sees eternal, unchanging symbols. Behind the spasmodic, frequently inconsistent activities of living men, he plainly distinguishes the great currents that sweep away the human soul. He takes ephemeral events and relocates them in an undying atmosphere. The great artist considers realistic representation a disfigurement and caricature of the eternal.

This is why not only the sculptors but all the great artists of classical Greece, wishing to ensure the perpetuation of every contemporary memorial to victory, relocated history in the elevated and symbolic atmosphere of myth. Instead of representing contemporary Greeks warring against the Persians, they gave us the Lapithae and centaurs. Behind the Lapithae and centaurs we discern the two great, eternal adversaries: mind and beast, civilization and barbarism. Thus a historic event, occurring at a specific time, escaped time and bound itself to the entire race and that race's ancient visions. Last of all, it escaped the race and became an undying, panhuman memorial. By means of this symbolic ennoblement the Greek victories were thus elevated into those of all mankind.

All this applies as well to the twelve metopes that embellished the temple of Zeus. They represent the twelve feats of Heracles. Even in the shattered, ruinous state in which they were preserved for us and hung here on the museum walls, how deeply they move us, to what proud heights they elevate the mind! Look how Athena, the human intellect, young as yet but full of vigor, stands by the athlete and aids him. In a similar way, a short while earlier, she must have leaped from the Acropolis to Marathon and Salamis in order to help the Greeks. Further along on the metopes she is seated upon a rock, a little fatigued from her efforts, but proud. Look how she gazes at the athlete as he returns in triumph and offers her the birds of Stymphalus as spoils! Still a little further along, see how tenderly she lifts her hand as, standing behind him, she helps him support the weight of the world.

Though the artist surely wished to hymn the Greeks of his own time, he transferred the praise respectfully to Heracles, the great ancestor and racial chieftain. The hymn seems to be saying, We of this generation did not attain the victory, it was attained by the genius of the race. It was attained by our forebear the obstinate, resolute athlete. Thus symbolically formulated, the hymn expands still further until it embraces the entire species of free man. We Greeks did not attain the victory, it says; it was attained not by our race alone, but by every man who, advancing from exploit to exploit, struggled to conquer beasts, barbarians, and death.

I passed through the museum door and walked a little way onto the pine-shaded patio. Here I was seized by sudden despondency. Would we moderns, I wondered, ever in our turn achieve the balance and the serene, heroic vision of the ancient Greeks? Every pilgrim, after he disengages himself from this Olympic dream, after he emerges through the museum door and faces the sun of our own day, surely, and with anguish, must pose this basic question to himself. For us Greeks, however, the despondency is twofold, because we consider ourselves descendants of the ancients. Thus, willy-nilly, we give ourselves the duty to equal our great ancestors—and even beyond this, every son's duty to surpass his parents.

How pleasant if the Greek could stroll through his country and not hear stern, angry voices beneath the soil! For the Greek, however, a journey through Greece degenerates into a fascinating and exhausting torture. You stand on a spot of Greek land and find yourself overcome with anguish. It is a deep tomb with layer upon layer of corpses whose varied voices rise and call you—for the voice is the one part of the corpse that remains immortal. Which among all these voices should you choose? Each is a soul, each soul yearns for a body of its own, and your heart listens, greatly troubled. It hesitates to make a decision, because the dearest souls are often not the most deserving.

I remember feeling this terrible, age-old struggle between heart and mind one noontime when I stopped beneath a blossoming oleander along the Eurotas, halfway between Sparta and Mistra. My unrestrainable heart charged forward to resuscitate the pallid, death-sealed body of our Byzantine emperor Constantine Palaeologus; to turn back the wheel of time to January 6, 1449, when here on the heights of Mistra he accepted the short-lived, blood-dyed crown of Byzantium. Innumerable ancestral gasps, innumerable racial yearnings prod us to follow our heart's desire, but the mind callously resists. Turning its face angrily toward Sparta, it wishes to toss the pallid emperor into the Kaiadas of time and cohere to the callous Spartan youths—for the mind's wish is precisely what this terrible moment demands of us, the terrible moment in which it was our lot to be born. If we want our lives to bear fruit, we must make the decision which harmonizes with the fearsome rhythm of our times.

When a Greek travels through Greece, his journey becomes converted in this fatal way into a laborious search to find his duty. How is he to become worthy of our ancestors? How can he continue his national tradition without disgracing it? A severe, unsilenceable responsibility weighs heavily on his shoulders, on the shoulders of every living Greek. The name itself possesses an invincible, magical force. Every person born in Greece has the duty to continue the eternal Greek legend.

In the modern Greek no region of his homeland calls forth a disinterested quiver of aesthetic appreciation. The region has a name; it is called Marathon, Salamis, Olympia, Thermopylae, Mistra, and it is bound up with a memory: here we were disgraced, there we won glory. All at once the region is transformed into much-wept, wide-roving history, and the Greek pilgrim's entire soul is thrown into turmoil. Each Greek region is so soaked with successes and failures possessing worldwide echoes, so filled with human struggle, that it is elevated into an austere lesson that we cannot escape. It becomes a cry, and our duty is to hear this cry.

Greece's position is truly tragic; on the shoulders of every modern Greek it places a duty at once dangerous and extremely difficult to carry out. We bear an extremely heavy responsibility. New forces are rising from the East, new forces are rising from the West, and Greece, caught as always between the two colliding impulses, once more becomes a whirlpool. Following the tradition of reason and empirical inquiry, the West bounds forward to conquer the world; the East, prodded by frightening subconscious forces, likewise darts forward to conquer the world. Greece is placed in the middle; it is the world's geographical and spiritual crossroads. Once again its duty is to reconcile these two monstrous impulses by finding a synthesis. Will it succeed?

It is a sacred and most bitter fate. At the end of my trip through Greece I was filled with tragic, unexpected questions. Starting with beauty, we had arrived at the agonies of our times and the present-day duty imposed on every Greek. Today, a man who is alive—who thinks, loves, and struggles—is no longer able to amble in a carefree way, appreciating beauty. The struggle, today, is spreading like a conflagration, and no fire brigade can ensure our safety. Every man is struggling and burning along with all humanity. And the Greek nation is struggling and burning more than all the rest. This is its fate.

The circle closed. My eyes filled with Greece. It seems to me that my mind ripened in those three months. What were the most precious spoils of this intellectual campaign? I believe they were these: I saw more clearly the historic mission of Greece, placed as it is between East and West; I realized that her supreme achievement is not beauty but the struggle for liberty; I felt Greece's tragic destiny more deeply and also what a heavy duty is imposed on every Greek.

I believe that immediately following my pilgrimage through Greece I was ripe enough to begin the years of maturity. It was not beauty that led the way and ushered me into manhood, it was responsibility.

This was the bitter fruit I held in my hand when, returning after my three-month journey, I entered my father's house.

Translated by P. A. Bien

Mycenae

Ilias Venezis

MANY YEARS AGO in faraway Anatolia, surrounded by perennial trees and isolated from the world, Katerina Pallis, a noble woman of the region, had withdrawn with her little boy to live on the property of her ancestors. She was still very young when her husband died, their son had just been born, and she assumed alone the task of preparing this child for true manhood. From the time he was little, she taught him to love the earth and the sun, to respect the labor of others, and to believe that a conscience is vindicated only by one's deeds. When he was a child, she would lull him to sleep with legends that told of distant lands, of places lashed by strong winds and tempests, of seafaring men who battle all their lives against the cold and the water and the phantoms of the sky. Their gaze is capable of rending the night, and their ear of seizing sounds brought by the wind from miles away. They worship the lightning that inscribes fire on the dark; they have rough hands; and like their bodies, their hearts are also lashed by violent winds. But in the hour of Judgment, those hearts come forth pure and spotless, because they performed their duty in life, having fought hard and suffered much.

This is how young Philip was raised. When he was old enough to understand and ask questions, Katerina Pallis spoke to him about his father. This was also like a legend that lasted many nights. In a warm voice, she attempted to bring back to life the form of that unknown father, which slowly assumed shape out of uncertainty and came, serene and sacred, to enter their midst.

And when Philip became still older, and his mother thought he was ready to be told, she then spoke to him about Greece. It was winter, the trees in the forest wailed, and the starving jackals howled. Huge logs burned in the fireplace, the air was thick, and the heat rose in small waves toward the high ceiling while the child, wide-eyed, listened to stories about the gods of Olympus, about the ravines and islands of Greece. They were strange legends, all the ones describing those gods, manlike creatures, who played with the joy of life, hunted in the forests, fell in love and suffered. There was nothing cruel or ascetic about them, they were all-powerful, they governed the wind, fire, and lightning. Of man's splendor there was only one thing they did not possess: the splendor of death. They were immortal; that is, never once at some mystical hour did they experience the terrifying shudder, the sign from the other world, that which gives men the right to be helpless, great, and alone: the chill of the grave.

Beneath such gods lived the mythical heroes of the land of Greece: Agamemnon and Clytemnestra and Iphigenia. When, at one time, evil men from parts of Asia came and abducted Helen queen of Sparta, then the brave young men of the realm became very angry.

They said: "This cannot be; we must take back our queen!"

And all the women said to their husbands: "Do not forsake our queen all alone to the barbarians! She is a woman and is as helpless as a reed!"

The brave young men then armed their wooden seacrafts in order to set out on an expedition to the distant land of Troy. The spirits of the winds, however, were not well disposed, the sails would not swell, and the ships stood stuck to the beaches of Greece. The prophet consulted the spirits, and they replied that they desired the sacrifice of a maiden. Iphigenia, the maiden with the black hair and black eyes, the first maiden of the land, heard it and said: "This is my destiny."

She went of her own will and offered up her girlhood of sixteen years as a sacrifice to the spirits of the winds. Then a favorable wind blew, the sails swelled, and the ships set forth.

Katerina Pallis narrated the story of Mycenae to her son in this manner. The child became wrapped in thought as he listened to the marvelous legend, trying by himself to understand the significance of the sacrifice, the motive of the courageous acts, the power of the calm. Outside, the night was black as pitch and starless; the jackals howled; the earth of Anatolia, undepleted and virginal, was nourishing the worms and the seeds.

"Ah, when will spring come?" begged the boy. "Will we go to Greece then?" he asked, and his voice trembled, for within this journey that he had been promised for the spring lived all the legends and dreams, the adoration of gods and men, the sacred earth.

"Let spring come!" his mother reassured him. "Then we will go to Greece."

Spring came; Katerina Pallis took her son and they went to Greece. It was afternoon when they arrived at Mycenae. They were climbing the uphill road leading to the Acropolis of Mycenae on foot when they grew weary. They looked around them. There was nothing to see. Only the barren earth and Sarra, the austere mountain that covered the site of the tombs.

"Is it much farther?" the child asked his mother.

"I don't believe so," answered Katerina Pallis. "If you want, we can sit down."

Then they saw a herd of goats, led by a young herdsman, descending around the bend in the deserted road.

"Let's ask the herdsman," said his mother.

When he came closer, she asked: "Is it still a long way to Mycenae?"

The young herdsman looked puzzled.

"Mycenae . . . ?" he asked. "I don't know of any Mycenae near here!"

"How about all this land around here . . . what is it?" Katerina Pallis asked again.

"Ah, here? . . . This is the pastureland of my grandfather Kakavas!"

The boy from Anatolia then laughed with all his heart.

"See, Mother!" he said. "And here we are looking for the tombs of our ancient kings!"

But Katerina Pallis became even more grave and hastened her step.

It was then that he appeared at the top of the road.

An old man was descending, with heavy movements, erect and serene. His white beard wrapped his face in small ringlets, his cape was thrown over his shoulders, he was wearing a white, billowing kilt made of wool, and his face, baked by the sun, looked like bronze. A light wind was blowing and ruffling his hair, but his steady gait gave the finishing stroke of serenity to the entire image. He was a living incarnation of the ancient figures of the land, as recounted in books and statues.

"Look, look, Philip!" the mother said to her son. "See how Greece lives on . . ."

"It's true, Mother! It's true . . . ," he also said, deeply moved. "How strange it is . . ."

In the simplest manner, with an old herdsman who appeared and inscribed his image on the evening landscape of Mycenae, the legends of Olympus started to assume a vivid form—the expedition to Troy and Agamemnon and Iphigenia, the sacrificial daughter with the black hair.

The old man approached, waved his rod in the air, then lowered it and rested it on the ground. But he did not lower his head like the villagers and herdsmen in Anatolia. He looked them right in the eyes, his body straight as a tree.

"Welcome to our land!" he said. "You must be strangers."

This time Katerina Pallis did not ask if it was Mycenae. She merely said: "We are strangers, old man! Where are the tombs of your ancient kings?"

The old man, gesturing slowly, pointed behind him.

"Just beyond Sarra!" he said. "There is where you will find them!"

There, as night fell and the sea of Argos disappeared from their sight, there they found them. First they saw the large, arched, royal tomb of Agamemnon and they went inside. The earth, to preserve it these many thousands of years, had gathered above it, becoming a hill, sprouting grass and trees, bringing forth flowers until its hour should come to emerge again and be worshiped by men. Darkness and profound calm prevailed within. On a small altar, where the sanctuary or the place for offerings must have been, Katerina Pallis found a few dry twigs. They set fire to them, then waited and watched. Nothing. How desolate it was! Except that every once in a while, a little water dripped from the dome. The earth above gathered it, held it inside itself, sanctified it, and later allowed it to pass down through the hard rocks of the dome and confer upon the serenity of the tomb a sound—a message from the world and from eternity.

"How alone the great king is in here . . . ," the boy murmured.

Katerina Pallis pulled him away and they went out. They passed by the humble tomb of Clytemnestra. The boy said they ought to enter there also, but his mother refused. What could she say to him about Clytemnestra and about her horrible deed? What should she say to him? No, she refused.

"Let us go to the Acropolis," she said, and headed toward the uphill path.

When they reached the Gate of the Lions, a fear seized the boy's heart. He took hold of his mother's hand.

"Are you afraid?" Katerina Pallis asked. "The citadel has been deserted for thousands of years. The dead do not speak."

She spoke thus even though she was well aware that in Greece the dead, in fact, do speak.

Here the atmosphere was happier, simpler. There were no vaulted monuments. The graves were only slightly below the surface of the earth. Wildflowers, yellow and red, grew here and there.

The child bent down to pick one. Later, when they descended from the Acropolis, he asked to enter again the tomb of Agamemnon. And there, on the ashes of the altar, on the ashes of the burned twigs, he placed it with affection, a message of the joy from the outside world, so that Agamemnon would not be alone.

What a long time has passed since then, what a great many years!

Katerina Pallis is journeying again on foot, this time alone, all alone, climbing the road to Mycenae. Now it is not spring, as it was then. Heavy clouds hang over the Acropolis of the tombs. And she is dressed in black. Mourning seals her pale face, and her hair is white. Of all that she lived for and brought up, nothing remains. Everything was left back there, in the catastrophe of Anatolia. There the brave young man, whom from the time he was a child she had prepared to become a true man, to respect the labor of others, and to believe that a conscience is vindicated only by one's deeds, had also perished. What is the meaning now of the legends she used to tell him about faraway lands, about places lashed by strong winds and turbulent seas, about men with pure hearts who all their lives battle against the cold and the water and the phantoms of the sky. What is the significance of all that now . . .

Katerina Pallis enters the tomb of Agamemnon. The same tranquillity, identical with that of so many years ago. The same desolation and the silence of death. There are no longer any ashes on the small altar, nor even any twigs as before. Only water from the earth drips slowly from the dome, slowly, at irregular intervals.

"My son . . . ," the mother softly says. "My boy . . . ," she says again, and remembers the humble flower the boy brought from outside to place on the altar, so that Agamemnon would not be lonely.

"So that Agamemnon would not be lonely . . . ," she murmurs. "And you, my child, where might you now be . . . ?"

With her white head bowed, with slow, weary steps, she goes outside. She looks around. She casts her eyes nearby, on the other, humble tomb where Clytemnestra rests. They remain there. Remain. And then, only then, does she see, truly see, that tomb for the first time. She humbly directs her footsteps toward it. She goes inside. How silent it is in here as well, the silence of death! Slowly, the light disappears, time disappears, only shadows stir in the air. And from inside there, from the depths of the shadows, forms slowly emerge and become clearly discernible. There once lived a hardhearted king. He was called Agamemnon. The people in his kingdom moaned and groaned under his tyranny and poured out rivers of perspiration so that he could accumulate countless riches in his castle. His power and tyranny stretched as far as the eye could see, over the entire plain of Argos. At one time, travelers who had gone astray happened on these parts. From their mouths Agamemnon learned that at the other end of the sea, toward Anatolia, in a wealthy land, Priam reigned, hoarding countless treasures in his castle—gold and much copper, herds of livestock and women the color of wheat and with sparkling eyes.

Agamemnon's mind became inflamed. Without delay he sent messages to the neighboring kings of the Arcadians, and they decided at once to launch the expedition to Troy. The entire army gathered on the beach of Aulis to embark. But a favorable wind would not blow. They waited for days, for weeks. Finally the prophet consulted the stars. And the stars said that if the angry gods were to be appeased, Agamemnon must offer as a sacrifice Iphigenia, the maiden with the black hair and black eyes. The king hesitated for a moment, but for a moment only. Then he thought of the herds of livestock and the gold and the copper and the slaves in the distant land, which was at the other end of the sea. His mind became muddled and he no longer hesitated. He sent a message for his wife to come, bringing his child. And there, beside the waveless sea, he surrendered with his own hands the maiden with the black hair, Iphigenia, to the executioner. The wind then blew, taking with it the fast-moving ships and the lamentations of Clytemnstra. And the land was filled with her wailing and curses.

For years Clytemnestra waited for Agamemnon to return from the foreign land, for years she brooded over her dreadful revenge. One of her slaves stood sentry every day, from dawn to dusk, to sight the much-traveled ships. Until one day the slave arrived breathless and fell at her feet, bringing the momentous news: "He's coming! Agamemnon is coming!"

Clytemnestra withdrew to her chambers; for a long time she remained alone praying to the gods. She did not cry. She only beseeched them to come to her aid in this sacred hour when a mother would perform her supreme duty. Next she calmly went out to the Gate of the Lions, determination flashing in her eyes. She sent for Aegisthus to stand by her, should her hand tremble at the last moment.

Agamemnon arrived, dragging behind him herds of slaves and cattle from the plunder of Troy. Next to him, Cassandra, Priam's daughter, followed barefooted. Clytemnestra led him to the bath. She gave him aromatic oils with which to anoint himself and, as soon as he had bathed, she threw a large sheet over his face. And at the same time as he was drying himself, Clytemnestra raised the ax and split his head. Afterward she sent for Cassandra. And she butchered her with her own hands next to the blood-stained body of Agamemnon, as he had butchered their child Iphigenia next to her.

Night is falling when Katerina Pallis emerges from the tomb of Clytemnestra.

The weather is oppressive, the black clouds collide with one another in the sky. They touch the top of the naked mountain, Sarra, and hasten away from it, as if there were danger that it might detain them. Its bulk rises dimly, a dark divinity that waits.

Katerina looks around her. After a time her bitter gaze falls to the ground with calm resignation—the refuge of people who have suffered greatly.

Then she sees it at her feet. It is a poor, lonely, yellow flower of the earth. How is it able to endure there, in the dreadful solitude, how?

She bends down and plucks it. Afterward, slowly, performing the same action her son performed so many years before—before they took him from her hands—but now in a different spirit, she comes and lays it on the deserted tomb of Clytemnestra, so that a mother, the mother of Iphigenia, will not be alone.

Translated by Nicholas Kostis

Panayotis

Thanassis Valtinos

HE WAS BORN IN KYNOURIA, in the village of Kara-
toula. He was drafted in 1919. In the fall of 1920, after a
year's delay, he was called up for duty in the army.

He reported for duty at Nafplion, right after the November elections—the elections that Venizelos lost—in the reg-
iment of the Eighth Infantry Battalion. They kept him
there for three months, taught him to use a machine gun,
and sent him off, via Piraeus, to fight in Asia Minor.

There, between March and July of 1920, he took part in
the fighting in Eski Sehir—and was decorated for it.

(The victorious Commander Konstantinos himself, "son
of the Eagle," paused before him in ancient Dorylaion and
pinned the medal on his chest.)

Two weeks later, at the age of twenty-three, during army
maneuvers leading up to the decisive attack, he went across
the Salt Desert, on an all-day, all-night, stinking, sweat-
filled trek, with no water but with excellent morale, all the
way to Gordion. They were heading for the "Red Apple
Tree" in the Turkish heartland.

When the front collapsed, in 1922, miles and miles away
from the Sangarios River, in Ali Veran, he was taken pris-

oner along with General Trikoupis and the rest of the men from the Third Army Corps.

It was their final battle.

At the Ousak prison camp the survival rate was one out of three and, after hammering rocks down to gravel for eighteen months, he found his way to Cilicia.

During the exchange of 1924, altogether unexpectedly, he was taken down to Smyrna with about three hundred other men.

A Red Cross committee was waiting for them at the station at Basma Hane, and they were gathered en masse and loaded onto a steamship, the *Marika Toyia*, which was leaving from the Iron Steps of Pounta. As it set sail Panayotis, standing on the highest deck, watched the land behind him grow smaller.

Despite all the humiliation he had been through and despite the rags he was covered in, he continued to have an angelic quality about him.

It was much later that his illness first appeared, at the end of 1927. His right hand began to shake, it was something like Parkinson's disease. He also began to stutter. The doctors who examined him were of the opinion that it was due to the hardships of captivity.

An old war buddy of his, a party boss, urged him to apply for a pension. He helped him to fill out the papers. They sent them to the ministry and waited. Nine months later he received a negative answer.

In the meantime, his mother died and so did an older brother of his who had been supporting them both.

For a long time, to make ends meet, Panayotis ran errands for people. Then he was forced to start begging, which he did in his own peculiar way; he would gather dried herbs, like oregano or sage, and sell them, in minute quantities—just a pretext for maintaining whatever pride he still had left.

A seamstress from his neighborhood, a onetime childhood sweetheart of his, now married, felt sorry for him and sewed him up a set of calico bags, with pleats at the top. He would fill them patiently, load them on his back, and walk the streets with them. That was how he became known to practically everyone in the Peloponnesus: Panayotis.

Sometimes on the highways, in the heat of summer, some wise-guy truck drivers would stop and pick him up, let him ride next to them, and say the most awful things to him—just to have some fun during their trip.

Even the bums in the small towns where he stayed overnight would make fun of him. Sometimes they tied cans on him and sometimes bits of paper that they would set on fire.

He accepted it all, not like someone resigned to his fate, but good-naturedly. Perhaps deep down he, too, enjoyed it.

In 1957, on my way down from Macedonia, while on furlough, I ran into him in Argos, at a brothel. Trying to sell fertility herbs to the women. We were distant relatives through marriage, and when he saw me he turned red with embarrassment. He must have been almost sixty then. In 1973 he retired permanently to his village. He was old by then, he was losing his eyesight, and his legs were no longer strong enough to carry him around like they used to. Some nieces of his took him in. They gave him his meals and one of them laundered his only change of clothing for him every other week. In return, he would take the two or three goats they kept in their cellar out to pasture.

He died that same year, in the month of August. He had taken the animals out to graze, felt thirsty, and bent down to drink from some water hole, lost his balance, and drowned—in only four inches of water.

Translated by Jane Assimakopoulos

The Hole in the Rock

Leonidas Zenakos

THE COFFIN LEANED dangerously, placed as it was on uneven ground in the stony courtyard. I wondered if it were nailed shut, and if it were not, what would happen if it keeled over. All around it, under the lattice of the grape-vine, these crazy quilts had been spread out where the meal for the dead was given. When I arrived at the house of the blessed departed in a far-off Piraeus neighborhood, the feast had ended; relatives and friends, all dressed in black, had just gotten up off the ground and were loosening their limbs to take out the numbness. Women in black dresses with black kerchiefs over their bent heads were picking up the leftover food; lilting notes of a dirge were in the air, ever so low, and I couldn't tell which of the women was doing the singing, nor could I make out the words. Just outside the gate a yellow minibus waited.

They offered me roast lamb with potatoes and red wine. I had no taste for food. I drank the wine, and, as the scene somewhat disturbed me, I took to observing it closely. But they soon invited me to take an active role: to help in trans-ferring the coffin from the courtyard to the minibus, together with three other close relatives.

The turmoil that overcame me was justifiable, and of course, it was responsible for the awkward incident that followed.

Halfway to our destination, entirely unexpectedly—or rather, after a momentary pause—the drone of the dirge singer rose suddenly to a powerful heartrending howl, which one would think made the surrounding hills shudder; in the event, that's what it did to me. Though I had my wits about me enough to discern the characteristic simplicity of the couplet, "Go, Father, and Godspeed / greetings to those below," still my arms went limp, and the coffin fell from my hands and thundered against the stones of the courtyard, while the other three continued to hold onto it, leaning as it was on the ground. Fortunately, it did not open; it really was nailed down.

A silence fell—a deadly silence, what else? All eyes were on me. My guilt was profound, and it took enormous courage to bend down and lift the coffin again.

Shortly the yellow minibus, with the coffin tied on the rack above and with a handful of relatives inside, started out for the hometown of the deceased, where the burial would take place. I stood there and watched it follow the dirt road downhill, raising a cloud of dust and adding yet one more to my many canceled trips to Mani—the one most marked, as it would prove some years later. I watched it go and I kept thinking about the implacable aunt Barbara.

Quite a few years before this incident, during the Civil War in the late 1940s, left-wing guerrillas had murdered two of my aunt Barbara's sons, practically beardless boys both. Aunt Barbara had wailed and sung their dirges for hours on end, as was fitting; then she returned to her home from the cemetery with dried eyes and tight lips. And there she opened the ancient chest, took out her dead husband's old shotgun, and hung it up on the nail next to the door: Aunt Barbara would wait until she happened upon a male offspring of "the others" to exact her revenge.

"The others" were of course the few who made up the weak leftist branch of the whole line of descendants. This bleak prospect hung over them for years to come. Many boys were born under the chill of its shadow. Mani was to be forbidden territory, especially for the young; as for the old ones, eventually some would return in a minibus, yellow or some other color.

But the years had passed and Greece became peaceful again. Aunt Barbara's shotgun was mentioned less and less. Eventually, those who even brought up the subject would turn it into a joke. Still, I never ceased to detect in those conversations a certain disturbing remnant of something.

In the end, Aunt Barbara died. Only her third son, a middle-aged man by then, and some of her nephews had stayed in the village; it was widely assumed in the family that the matter of revenge had closed with her death. But was this assumption shared by everyone? I wondered.

At about this time, I, like so many others, was taken by an irresistible urge to get to know the place of my origins; not that I could claim I was attracted by my roots, as they say, but more likely I, too, was the victim of tourist propaganda, which at that time, and rather unexpectedly, favored Mani.

My trip was short. Perhaps that's why in thinking about it now there remains, as something fleeting and dreamlike, the aura of the landscape, a grotesque mixture of coarseness and tempering: the threatening architectural oddity of the famous towers, the tiny spectral southernmost port, at once dangerous and primordially secure, the rich light, pale, sweet, yet painfully penetrating. Or perhaps it is the nature of Mani to seem evanescent and intangible, even though it is so intensely real and undeniably there.

And then again, I recall vividly almost every detail of the trip that concerned me personally.

The village was deserted; a few of its inhabitants had remained, but even they lived by the new shops along the main thoroughfare, the road that buses full of tourists followed to reach the caves. Walking through the narrow streets, between the high stone walls of the houses, I did not encounter a living soul. I came upon memories, however, even though secondhand ones, strangely moving confirmations of descriptions and narratives I had listened to, enraptured, long ago: such as the highest window of the village, in the tallest stone wall, always shut (even now)— except when somebody would dare to reach up and pick a mulberry from the tree opposite, then the window would open, ever so slightly, just enough to admit the barrel of a shotgun; the huge rock rooted dead center in the path, which served as a kind of village notary—it would be enough for the parties to an agreement to step on it with their right foot for the contract to be sealed; the corner of the debauched daughter, the spot where her father-lover had stabbed her to death when he found out that she was also giving herself to her brother and his son; the ledge where chaff was discarded from the prickly pear trees; and finally, the house of Aunt Barbara.

In the beginning I didn't mind the solitude, but as twilight set in a kind of gloom weighed heavy in the atmosphere. The bleakness of the hour, together with my exhaustion after so many hours of driving, no doubt played its part in my strange psychic state, which resembled a kind of expectant awe, as I climbed the high stone stairs of Aunt Barbara's house. Like all the other houses, it, too, was closed shut, standing next to an enormous fig tree. I reached the little wooden double door with the panes of glass on its upper half and the tiny curtains on the inside.

I can't imagine what I was after when I pressed my face to the glass, peering through the opening in the curtains; by now the light had all but disappeared and I saw nothing, or nearly nothing. Baffled, I removed my face from the glass. Could it be, after all these years? There wasn't the slightest sound anywhere, only the momentary rustle of the fig leaves in the light wind. I leaned toward the pane of glass again; I couldn't be sure. It could've been anything, or nothing at all, simply a long shadow on the wall next to the door.

I descended the stairs rather quickly.

I'd hardly taken ten paces on my way out of the village when I crossed paths with a middle-aged man dressed in black. He uttered a heartfelt good evening, and I returned his greeting with great politeness—in an exaggerated fashion, perhaps. In the half darkness I could not make out his face, but I heard the jingling of keys in his hand; he was on his way to get something from some house. What, I wondered, and from which house?

It seems this thought of mine struck a bargain with the mosquitoes at the small hotel, for together they prevented me from shutting an eye that whole night. Possibly something else bothered me even more: the hotel receptionist, a native of Mani, was a bit overly expressionless as he returned my I.D. card. Especially since my surname is not unknown in these parts.

There was a time when the now famous Caves of Mani—the area's main tourist attraction—were not even caves. Before they were excavated and developed into a sightseeing spot there used to be, so they say, a place where brackish water flowed from the rock to the sea. There was a hole in the rock through which one could see or hear the water underneath. Children would dive into the hole, swim through the water under the rock, and reach the open sea. The more daring ones would even swim in the opposite direction. But no one had ever found the origins of these subterranean waters.

I was moving in just that direction underneath the mountain the following morning, about a mile in from shore, in a shallow boat so overloaded with tourists that its gunwale was no more than a few inches from the sleek, dark, crystalline water of the subterranean lake. The ferryman, rowing gently from aft, often interrupted his sightseeing speech to remind us not to make any sudden movements; the water, extremely cold, was quite deep, he said, and we would shortly be reaching the deepest point: one hundred and eighty feet.

I thought to myself that I would not like it one bit if I found myself in these waters. I wasn't afraid I might drown —I know how to swim—it was rather something deeper, almost metaphysical, something suggested by those weird surroundings, those stalactites and stalagmites with their strange shapes and colors, made even more imposing by the artful lighting against the heavy rock dome of the vast cave.

The spectacle had absorbed me entirely, as it had the rest of the passengers. I kept turning my head in all directions —being exceedingly careful with my movements—so that I wouldn't miss anything of this singular beauty, all the while listening to the series of informative points the ferryman was making, but without looking in his direction. It was only when he announced that we had reached the point of maximum depth that I fixed my eyes upon him, without knowing why. Next to him, on the bench in the stern, was seated a middle-aged man in black; he was eyeing me, unwavering, though it's true I sat directly opposite, in his line of vision, at the prow. Was it indeed the same man? I wondered.

Regardless of what I believe today, then I took the answer to my question to be the almost fatal incident that occurred only a few minutes later. We were on our way back, and already I could make out in the distance the light spilling into the docking station—the reason why there were no more lighting devices and we were moving in half darkness. Just then the middle-aged man in black stood up and made as if to come in my direction, that is, toward the prow. The boat rocked precariously, it almost capsized; shrieks from women and children echoed inside the rock dome, and the ferryman shouted at the unruly passenger that he shouldn't be in such a hurry, everyone would disembark in good time, and he should wait his turn. He sat down heavily in his place again without uttering a word.

A certain anxiety pervaded the small vessel; everyone

looked at the bright opening with longing. Everything stopped—the exclaiming, the admiring of the scenery, the comments, the laughter. There was only silence. In the few minutes that remained of the excursion, women pulled their children toward them in a hug; men, in disquiet, looked at the rocks around them, then down, or rather beside them, at the black water. The ferryman, now speechless, had speeded up his rowing. And I couldn't help but wonder how I had come—without intending it, of course —to have innocent lives on my head. When at last we came alongside the dock and climbed the glistening steps, I looked around to see the middle-aged man in black. He had vanished.

That afternoon in the hotel, again I could not sleep, I was even more restless than the night before. Lying there half drowsing, I tried in vain to set things straight, objectively, and to decide if I really had reason to worry or if perhaps all these events that seemed to me ill-omened were nothing but untrustworthy associations of a cultivated imagination firmly in place for years.

Hunger pulled me out of my lethargy. I'd gone for a while without food, and now it was night.

The dimly lit restaurant was on the road to the caves. At that hour the surrounding landscape, with the gentle hills drenched in moonlight and the sea flickering beyond, was pure magic. The place had hardly any business. In its ample gravel-strewn courtyard only one table was taken; a small party, all men, was having a quiet conversation about dogs and prey—they were anxious for the hunting season to arrive.

I sat at a table and surrendered to the merciful coolness

of the night air after the day's scorching heat. I ordered, and by the time the food came I'd already downed several shots of ice-cold ouzo. I went at the fresh mullet and the tomato salad with the local, aromatic olive oil ravenously, following it up with a tender pork chop, fried potatoes, and delicious sausages, also locally made.

I was on my fruit course, chilled watermelon, when the moon set behind the hills; the place had gone gradually dark. Perhaps that's why I didn't notice that the company at the other table had increased by one. First I saw the long canvas case on the chair, which had not been there before, the shape of which left no doubt as to its contents; then I noticed the new arrival, who at that moment was reaching his hand toward the case. He was middle aged and he was wearing black.

On the main road, a thick darkness had succeeded the bright moonlight; the car's headlights seemed unable to penetrate it. I was driving carefully, but also as fast as I could. Anguish and an urgent need to sleep were struggling inside my wildly upset brain—it wasn't a good idea to have drunk so much ouzo, I thought, tormented as I was by doubts over whether it really was necessary to leave Mani so soon. I was trying once more to put my thoughts into some order, but the disturbing, uninvited memories, all jumbled up, left me no room for calm thinking.

I drove like this for quite a while, and every so often I would check the rearview mirror to see if I was being followed. The road was deserted, but maybe it was because of my distracted mind that I suddenly found the yellow minibus in front of me. I stepped abruptly on the brakes and I heard for what seemed a very long time the screeching of the tires before I hit it—very gently, it is true.

I want to believe that I shut my eyes at that precise moment, but perhaps by then they were already shut. In any case, I opened them and got out. My car had stopped at a small opening by the side of the road and its front bumper was ever so lightly touching the bark of an olive tree. There was no minibus: I badly needed sleep, for sure. I got back into the car, shut off the headlights, adjusted the seat, and lay down, covering myself with a blanket.

I was awakened by the sun, already scorching hot. The landscape around me, ineffable and serene, suggested nothing of the previous evening's nightmare. An olive grove stretched out to my right, ending at the foot of a hillside in the distance. To my left was the road; next to it extended flat rocks and below them the sea, smooth, like a mirror.

I got out of the car, crossed the road, and descended to the rock. In front of me I saw a hole—it was almost three feet in diameter—and below it, the water. This must be a common phenomenon in these parts, I said to myself. I took off my clothes down to my briefs. Then I wriggled carefully into the hole and, when my feet touched the water, let myself dive softly in. I swam under the rock, underwater, and came out in the deep-green sea.

Translated by John Chioles

Delphi

George Seferis

IN THE BEGINNING was the wrath of the earth. Later, Apollo came and killed the chthonic serpent, Python. It was left to rot. It is said that this is where the first name of Delphi, Pytho, came from. In such a fertilizer the power of the god of harmony, of light, and of divination took root and grew. The myth may mean that the dark forces are the yeast of light; that the more intense they are, the deeper the light becomes when it dominates them. One would think that if the landscape of Delphi vibrates with such an inner radiance, it is because there is no corner of our land that has been so much kneaded by chthonic powers and absolute light.

Descending toward Parnassus from the direction of the Stadium, one sees the wide-open wound that divides, as if by a blow of Hephaestus's ax, the two Phaedriades ("shining rocks") from top to bottom in Castalia and, even lower, to the depths of the ravine of Pleistos. One feels the awe of a wounded life that struggles in order to breathe, as long as it still can, in the light, and rejoices that it is dawn and the sun is rising.

Or again, as night falls, when the weary cicadas become

silent, a whisper can remind one of the stammering voice of the prophetess Cassandra. It may be the only authentic sound that resembles to us the unknown—I mean "un-processed"—"clamor" of Pythia:

woe, woe, woe! O Apollo, O Apollo!
(Aeschylus, *Agamemnon*, 1072)

Cassandra had the gift of prophecy, as they say, but God wanted nobody to believe her; as we ourselves do not believe her.

As one comes from Athens to Delphi, after Thebes and Livadia, where the road meets the road to Daulis, there is the crossroads of Megas, the "bandit-killer," as he was called in the popular novels of the last century. In the years of Pythia, this crossroads was called "split road." It was a very significant crossroads for the emotional complexes of the people of those days; maybe, in another way, for us too. There begins the story of Oedipus, who answered the Sphinx; of the blind Oedipus, the ultimate suppliant. Pythia had given her oracle to his father: "Laius, you ask me for a son; I will give him to you; but it is your fate that from his hands you will lose the light of day." Laius was going to Delphi; Oedipus was returning. They met at this crossroads under the heavy mass of Parnassus. Neither of the two knew whom he was facing. They argued. Oedipus killed his father.

We are living in a technological age, as we say. Pythia has vanished; and out of the myth of Oedipus science has drawn symbols and terms that occupy us perhaps more

than the Oracle of Delphi occupied the ancients. Today
this tale may still give many people a pleasant evening at
the theater, if it happens, by chance, that a good actor is
performing. But if we do not have that Oedipus, we have
the Oedipus complex and its consequences. Is it better this
way? Maybe. The problem is not so much which things
have come to an end but with what we—who are living, like
everything in life, amid decay and change—replace those
things we consider finished.

I am thinking of those big waves from the depths of time
that shift the meaning of words. For example, the meaning
of the word *oracle:* Where has it gone today? The word
became an archaeological object. Agreed. But its meaning?
Could it possibly have taken on, imperceptibly, a particular
scientific or mathematical form? Who knows. However,
what one feels is that in the depths of today's thought something must have remained of the old, abolished expressions.
Otherwise how could we feel such a vibration here?

One can also go to Delphi from the direction of the sea,
from Itia. It used to be called Kirra, and there Apollo, transformed into a dolphin, brought the Minoan ship. Thus
Pytho was named Delphi, if we believe the Homeric hymn:

> and in as much as at the first on the hazy sea
> I sprang upon the swift ship in the form of a dolphin,
> pray to me as Apollo Delphinius; also the altar itself
> shall be called Delphinius and overlooking forever.
>
> ("To Apollo," 493ff.)

It is nice to start from the seashore and enter among the
olive trees under the silver leaves of the plain of Criseos,

enumerating, as you pass by, the wrinkles on the dense gathering of trunks; and if by any chance this shadow weighs heavily upon you and you raise your eyes, you suddenly see, in the perpetually moving blue, the twin peaks of Parnassus; further down you see the extension of the western Phaedriad, and even lower down the acropolis of Crisa. Around there the chariot races that were praised by Pindar took place. There is this rhythm that breathes, along with two or three other stark voices, over Delphi:

> . . . neither by ships nor by land canst thou find
> the wondrous road to the trysting-place of the
> > Hyperboreans
> > > (Pindar, *Pythian Odes,* X, 29ff.)

It is said that Apollo used to go to the Hyperboreans for three months every year. Who were the Hyperboreans? They have sunk into myth. At their table—Pindar continues—Perseus sat one day. He saw them sacrifice excellent hecatombs of asses to the god; Apollo was laughing as he looked at the erect shamelessness of the beasts that were offered to him. The Muse is always with them; neither sickness nor age touches this sacred race; they do not need to work hard; they do not have fights. They have escaped the avenger Nemesis.

Up there in Delphi, after you pass the village and reach the temple, you have the feeling that you have entered a place separate from the rest of the world. It is an amphitheater nestling on the first steps of Parnassus. From the east and the north it is closed by the Phaedriades: Hyambeia, which descends like the prow of a big ship and cuts the ravine; the northern Rodini, which almost touches the

Stadium. From the western side, the rocky wall of Saint Elias, and further down the mountains of Locrida, Giona, where you see the sun set. If you turn your eyes to the south, you have in front of you the robust lines of Cirphis, and at its foot the ravine of Pleistos. Pleistos is dry in the summer; you see its dry bed shine in the sun, but a river of olive trees is streaming, you would say, flooding the whole plain of Amphissa, all the way down to the sea where the seafarer sees them for the first time. Close by, the shiny stones of the ruins of Marmaria, where the three columns of Tholos jut out. I almost forgot Castalia. However, its water has a fragrance of thyme.

The temple of Apollo is reckoned to be approximately two hundred meters in depth and one hundred thirty in width, not including the Stadium. The space is not very large, and it is natural that the monuments, as they were crowded here, had to develop vertically in order to grow taller than the others: think of the Sphinx of Naxos, the column with the dancers, the snakes of Plataia. One tries to imagine all these as they were when they breathed intact. They must have looked, from a distance, like cypresses, shiny, multicolored, around the temple of Pythia. One just tries. What comes to mind is the dawn that Ion saw; as far as the natural landscape is concerned, this dawn is, I think, conventional, but it reflects, I feel, the brilliant splendor of the temple as one imagines it to have been in those years:

Lo, yonder the Sun-god is turning to earthward his
   splendor-blazing
   Chariot of light;
And the stars from the firmament flee from the fiery
   arrows chasing,

To the sacred night:
And the crests of Parnassus untrodden are flaming and
      flushed as with yearning
Of welcome to far-flashing wheels with the glory of
      daylight returning
   To mortal sight.
To the roof-ridge of Phoebus the fume of the incense of
      Araby burning
   As a bird taketh flight.
On the tripod most holy is seated the Delphian Maiden
Chanting to children of Hellas the wild cries, laden
      with doom, from the lips of Apollo that ring.
               (Euripides, *Ion,* 82ff.)

  One is still trying. The imagination grows tired. The retrospectives and the reconstructions, no matter how useful, become most inhuman. What else do we have from this "instantaneous present"? In the end, the imagination prefers that the river of time should have passed and filled this limited space. Today, looking down from above, let us say from the theater, you have the impression that you have before you a downward-sloping bottom where everything is leveled—these marble fragments and carved stones and the rocks which rolled in older times from Parnassus and on which Sibylla once sat; the bottom of a calm shallow sea where the pebbles shine, where everyone discerns as much as he can, depending on his nature: a polygonal wall so much alive that one's hand spontaneously repeats the movements of the craftsman who carved and fitted the stones, a bending of the thumb and the index finger to raise a dress with the same grace that one saw the other day in a Greek village; a lifelike thigh, as the knee of a woman descending from the chariot bends; the head of a Sphinx with the eyes neither open nor closed; a smile that one would call archaic —but this is not enough—of a Hercules or a Theseus. Such fragments from a life that was once whole, stirring pieces, very close to us, ours for a moment and then enigmatic and inaccessible like the lines of a stone licked smooth by the waves or of a seashell at the bottom of the sea.

Yet, the Phaedriades shine as does the dry rock of Parnassus, and higher up in the air two eagles with outstretched, immobile wings move slowly in the azure sky like the eagles that Zeus once set free so that they would show him the center of the world. Perhaps these things come as a big relief.

At noon, in the museum, I looked again at the Charioteer. He did not live long in the eyes of the ancients, so we are told. An earthquake buried the statue one hundred years after it was erected—this perpetual dialogue, in Delphi, between the wrath of the earth and sacred serenity. I stayed near him for a long time. As in older times, as always, this motionless movement stops your breath; you do not know; you are lost. Then you try to hold on to the details; the almond-shaped eyes with the sharp, transparent look, the strong jaw, the shadows around the lips, the ankle, or the toenails; the robe which is and is not a column. You look at its seams, the crisscrossed ribbons that hold it together; the reigns in his right hand that stay there, tangled, while the horses have sunk into the chasm of time. Then the analysis bothers you; you have the impression that you are listening to a language not spoken anymore. What do these details which are not artistry mean? How do they disappear like that within the whole? What was behind this living presence? Different ideas, different loves, a different devotion. We have worked like ants and like bees on these relics. How close have we come to the soul that created them? I mean this grace at its peak, this power, this modesty, and the things that these bodies symbolize. This vital breath that makes the inanimate copper transcend the rules of logic and slip into another time, as it stands there in the cold hall of the museum.

I chose to walk up to the Corycian Cave from the ancient path; it is too rough for today's habits: the animals slip. The rhythm of the mule's bell and of the horseshoes on the rocks is something from another time; this iamb.

It is dawn; from above, the Stadium looks as if it was built in the sand by a child; then what scares you is the big gaping wound of the Phaedriades. On the ridge of Cirphis you see the rosy shades of the houses in a village. It is Desfina; behind it, down at the seashore, with more golden shades, is Galaxidi. We get off the horses at Kroki, where a fountain is running and a flock of goats with twisted horns and black fur, shining in the light, are drinking water. In the old days these places were pastures—Dionysus: "goat thrower." (A temple of Dionysus bearing this name existed in Boeotia. According to legend, the name was given to the temple when Dionysus threw a goat to the altar to replace a boy who was about to be sacrificed.) Then we walk under the fir trees; their cones—people call them "rubala"—like the candles of a Christmas tree, shed tears of resin, which makes them look silvery. At the foot of the hill of Sarandavlio, as the cave is called today, we left the mules. Pausa-

nias is right. "Climbing up to the Corycian Cave is easier
for the pedestrian than for the mule or the horse," he tells
us. But even for the pedestrian the path is very rough. As
we climb up, I ask my mule driver if there are still fairies in
the cave, as I heard down in the village. He laughs; he does
not feel that fairies are appropriate for a modern man.
"Fairies in our times!" he says. Yet his denial seems to me
less sincere when he adds: "I myself never saw them"; and
after some silence he continues: "A foreigner told me that
here, in this cave, Apollo had forty beautiful weavers, gathered from the surrounding villages, who wove for him all
the time." It seems more probable to me that he heard the
story from his mother rather than a foreigner. A fellow villager of his told me the other day, down in Castalia: "And
these plane trees down here ate the ones that Agamemnon
himself planted." "Agamemnon?" I said in surprise. He
looked at me as if I was ignorant. "Of course Agamemnon,"
he said, "what did you think?"

Through Delphi passes a large crowd of tourists. "Delphi has become an endless hotel," a native told me. As in
Plutarch's time, I thought. I had remembered his dialogue
about Pythia's oracles. In those times too, the temple had
become a tourist place with organized guides showing the
sites to the crowds. The difference is that in Plutarch's time,
the people who visited Delphi still had, as a common tradition, a faith that was on the decline, as in Jerusalem in
our time. Today the common faith has been lost, and the
people who come each have different personal myths. They
reach or they listen to a guide; to this information each person adds his own. Among these various crowds, the people of Parnassus continue to live obstinately with the

traditional myths which their collective subconscious nurtures. (It is worth noting here one of the most charming: "The Milords are not Christians since nobody ever saw them make the sign of the cross. Their lineage comes from the old idolaters Adelphiotes, who kept their wealth in a castle and called it Adelphi (brothers) from the two brothers, sons of the king, who had built it. When the Virgin Mary and Christ came to these lands and the people all around became Christians, the Adelphiotes thought that it would be better for them to leave and they went to the land of the Franks, taking with them all their wealth. From those people the Milords are descended, and they now come and pay their respects to these stones.")

I wanted to climb to the Corycian Cave because I thought that this visit to the place of Apollo had to be completed with a feeling of Dionysus, whom Pythia supported so strongly—of the dead and alive god, the infant god; that emotional force which willed that the instincts of man not be spurned. In the plateau around the cave, the Thyiades and Maenades held their periodic nocturnal orgies—whatever that ecstatic outburst of women possessed by the god means for us today. I was thinking of that frustrated king, Pentheus (Euripides, *Bacchae*). I was afraid of the example of his tragedy; I said: better the frenzy of the Thyiades in the high solitudes of Parnassus than its substitutes in the contemporary boundless anthills that are our big capitals. I was thinking of our collective madnesses.

To the right, as you enter the cave, the stone is still preserved with the half-effaced sign to the god Pan and the Nymphs. Then you have the feeling that you have descended into a large womb. The ground is damp and slippery; stalagmites and stalactites can be discerned in the dim light; it feels cold after the heat and the panting of the climb. Only after you proceed further and turn around do you see the rays of the sun like a blessing as they enter, parallel, through the mouth of the cave, striking its walls with a rosy and green iridescence. You rejoice at being born again in the warmth of the sun, certainly not poorer; you know that there is still something behind these things.

At one time, Plutarch tells us, people from a foreign land came to Delphi to consult the oracle. The preliminary test with the goat, which would show if the day was auspicious, was performed so that Pythia would deliver her oracle. But the animal did not shiver when sprayed with cold water; the sign was not good. Yet the foreigners must have been important, and in order to please them the priests exceeded the proper limits, until the animal, wet all over, showed signs of shivering. Then Pythia came down to the altar of the temple, "unwilling and reluctant." As soon as she gave the first answers, Plutarch continues, the ferocity of her voice showed that she was possessed by an angry and mean spirit. She looked like a windswept ship. Finally, in a complete frenzy, with dreadful screams, she sprang toward the exit. The prophet Nikandros, the priests, and the foreigners fled in terror. Later they returned and carried away the still-frantic Pythia. She died a few days later.

This incident, they say, should be considered authentic— it happened in Plutarch's time, and the prophet Nikandros who witnessed it was his friend; it shows us that Pythia was still functioning in the first century. It also makes us return to the eternal question that all of us who have thought about the very significant role—religious, political, private —that the oracle played in ancient Greek life have asked ourselves: were all these oracles and prophecies fabrications and frauds of sly priests, or was there possibly real sincerity underlying those things, something that goes beyond our common sense?

Plutarch's narration should make us think that it was not very probable that the breakdown of a woman leading up to her death could be mere acting. Of course there were priests who interpreted Pythia's words—how articulate nobody knows—and delivered them, arranged in hexameters, trimeters, or prose, to the faithful; no doubt they were opportunists, shifty, cautious, masters of ambiguity. But as in our time, it is one thing to look at such matters of the soul from the point of view of God and another from that of his servants.

It has been said that the phenomenon of Pythia must be included in the phenomena of that which we call today *spiritualism*. Perhaps. In that case, though, the least one could remark is that Pythia resembles a contemporary medium as much as the Charioteer does a contemporary statue of mediocre art—let us say, of Jacob Epstein. This is the difference. By this I mean that in the sanctuary of Apollo there has remained a mystery that goes beyond us, just as in the art of the Charioteer. I don't know. What one can consider more clearly is that if the oracle did indeed stimulate Socrates' thinking, as Plato teaches us in the *Apology,* its contribution to the development of human thought would have been so great that it would have been worth founding for this reason alone.

Plutarch's narration approximately coincides with the event that brings to an end the world of the idols. Then the Oracle of Apollo slowly dries up, sparkling faintly, and, tired, finally disappears. Sometimes it whispers sentences that remind us of Sibylla's "I want to die," quoted by Petronius. Three hundred years or so have been spent among the wrinkles and the formal gestures of the clergy, who merely repeat and do not create. The only concern that seems to preoccupy them is the fear that the old habit of offering gifts to Apollo might come to an end. This until the ultimate answer of the Oracle to the tragic Julian:

> Tell the king the ornately designed temple has
> collapsed.
> Phoebus no longer has a home, nor a mantic
> laurel,
> nor a talking spring. The babbling water has
> run dry.

Yet, although the Oracle seems to write the last page of its history by itself and to descend into the grave of its own volition, the theoreticians of the new religion found it worthwhile to devote a lot of thought and ink to fighting it. The strange thing is that they do not set out to prove that such prophecies are the work of charlatans. They recognize the prophetic power of Delphi, but for them these things are the work of Satan and of the forces of darkness, and Apollo is a metamorphosed devil.

Here in Phocis, in the monastery of Saint Luke, a mosaic of Pantocrator, over the lintel of the west door, bears the inscription "I am the light of the world. He who follows me will not walk in darkness." Nature abhors a vacuum.

In the morning, at Marmaria, I went again to see the rocks that rolled down from Parnassus and destroyed the temple of Athena, as mentioned by Herodotus. In the beginning of our century, another storm again detached three large rocks and completed the destruction. The rocks are there among the trampled works of men, still showing, motionless now, their initial force. I remembered Angelos Sikelianos as he was listening to the onset of such a wind: "Not a sound is heard anywhere; and suddenly a horrendous roar, a strong and unbelievable roar breaks out as if from every direction. It is the great wind of Parnassus which starts up unexpectedly from the peaks toward the open spaces, with such force that you think it will shatter even the rocks to dust." The poet of Delphi—if any of our contemporaries can be called the man of Delphi—was writing in his house, high up near the Stadium, where I met him for the first time. His house is now in ruins; an ugly bust of him outside the door underlines the futility of glory.

As I was returning to the place where the round pool of the Gymnasium baths remains dry, five or six girls, very young, with legs naked up to above the knee, as if obeying a decision or an order, walked down very seriously, linked arms, and danced two or three rounds, singing in a Hyperborean language I did not know. Hyperborean girls, I suppose: the dances of the Hyperborean virgins of Pindar. Then, looking very serious and still panting, they approached a guide who started lecturing in English: "The gymnasium was not only for the training of athletes; philosophers taught the young, poets recited their poems, astronomers explained from this spot the movements of the stars in the sky . . ." In the evening, at about eleven o'clock, a friend showed me in the starry sky an artificial satellite that was moving from west to east with a discernible motion; it had the intensity of a star of second, or perhaps third, rank.

Like everything human and like the life of the stars, Apollo's Pythia had her beginning and also had her end in the wrath of the earth. "Phoebus has no home anymore." Now again it seems as if we have completed a cycle; we are again facing the wrath of the physical forces that we have set free and do not know whether we will be able to control them; one might say that we have in front of us a Python, that we need an Apollo, whatever these names mean. I don't know. What we know now is that the duration of this earth, as well as of this corner inside the loins of Parnassus, is relative—it may end tomorrow or after some million years; that when we say *eternity,* we do not have in mind something measured in years, but something like Pythia, who, when falling into a trance, saw the whole of space and the whole of time past and future as one thing. Or, to remember my friend E. M. Forster, *we must* call things *eternal,* in order to be able to struggle up to our last moment and to enjoy life. This sacred temple would probably whisper something like that to us.

If, however, we wish to look at things in a more simple and more direct manner, we could sit down on a stone at the time when the sun has passed the mountainous wall of Saint Elias and goes to set behind Giona. The light now comes parallel and strikes the Phaedriades, showing them like Clashing Rocks, stopped, half open. They are gray and light blue with the shades of an old mirror, with wounds of rust and blood. Down in Marmaria, three columns of the Tholos can be discerned, a smile of that earthly grace. Fur-

ther down, the olive trees keep changing color in the unbelievable flexibility of the light, from golden green to silver
green; the mountain masses also keep changing, always
becoming lighter: from golden to violet, from violet to the
color of crushed black grapes. Only the ridge of Cirphis
still shines in a saffron-colored light and stays alive for a
while before everything turns to light blue and then dark-
ens. You look again at the stairlike temple that is disappearing in the shadows, this seashore with the big broken
pebbles. You want to get away from it all. You want to get
away from this change—of things and feelings—that makes
you dizzy. You turn again toward the Phaedriades that you
looked at and looked at again throughout the day, and
especially at high noon, when they shine, dry, when the old
mirrors have found all their power again. The thought is
holding on to them, as long as it still can, to the dry stone
that refines you. No matter how much you resist, you cannot but have a feeling of sanctity about it. At least this: let
us be true to ourselves.

Translated by C. Capri–Karka

Galaxidi:
The Fate of a Maritime Town

Eva Vlami

GALAXIDI IS LOCATED on the mainland side of the
Corinthian Gulf. Tucked away in the folds of the land, it
is washed by the Krisaika waters, as the sea hidden in the
town's embrace is called. All around it is surrounded by tall
mountains, which grant it safety and shelter from the
winds. In truth, its bay is such that you would think it was
God's will for Galaxidi to become a maritime place. Long
ago the town was built on the mountainside. But one day,
one of the townspeople longed to go down to enjoy the sea,
which he saw stretched out carefree as far as the eye could
see. Soon after, someone else decided to join him, and
another followed, and thus the first families arrived. Upon
their arrival, they put up two or three wooden shacks and
started thinking of how to make a living.

At that time, they say, a sea nymph appeared one evening
near the shores of Galaxidi. The young men ran to see her.
But as soon as she became aware of them, she dived into
the sea, for she was stark naked. Charmed by her voice, the
young men toiled to build a boat. This done, they searched
the sea to find her, but they found nothing. They were

exhausted by their yearning and burned by the saltiness of the sea, but in vain. They did not find her anywhere. Then, one starlit night, the women of Galaxidi came down to the seashore and, facing eastward, they waited.

Just as a star caught fire and was about to be extinguished in the sea, they thought of her name: Galaxa. Unafraid this time, the nymph emerged from the water. The women of Galaxidi were amazed at her beauty. They fell to her feet so she would not bewitch their children. The nymph laughed, and her laughter poured balsam onto their soul. She explained to them that her father, Ocean, had sent her to this accommodating edge of the sea to bring the love of the sea to the hairy chests of the young men. Now that she had accomplished this, she would return to her depths, content, but the town would keep her name.

Once the first vessel was built, the men of Galaxidi did not waste time. They started fishing and transporting passersby to the opposite shore. In time they made other boats as well. So it became known that if you were in Roumeli and had to take care of some business across the Gulf of Corinth in the Moreas, good-natured and well-mannered men from Galaxidi could take you there on big boats. This brought money to the place, because merchants found it advantageous to come directly to Galaxidi instead of crossing to Patras, Egio, or wherever else they had to go in a roundabout way. Gradually, the men of Galaxidi brought home larger vessels from other places, and they ventured farther away.

In the beginning, they made trips to the Ionian islands, but as they became bolder they went out to the open seas to gather riches, secure the town, increase their number of

boats to match that of other places, and support their growing families as best they could. They also made the place
secure for their vessels and for the old people, women, and
children who stayed behind when the men left to go to sea:
they surrounded the town with walls and built a fortress at
the entrance of the bay.

The walls lasted until 1830, when what remained of them
was destroyed to make room for the pier. The place may
thereby have lost its greatness, I will not argue to the contrary; but the good thing that came out of this was that the
town could now expand freely along the shore and breathe
the air of the sea. Perhaps some of you have heard that outside the fortress of Galaxidi, built of skillfully chiseled marble slabs, many of its enemies were crushed: Bulgarians,
Huns, Normans, Franks, Spaniards, Turks. As the town's
prosperity was lauded everywhere, all these foreign plun-
derers wanted to make it their own. But they did not succeed. They merely harassed the townspeople.

For years the people of Galaxidi lived in the nearby villages, covering their nakedness with hides and nourishing
their bodies with hardly anything, for the land was very
infertile. And, if having always to be prepared for war were
not enough, many times sickness and death contaminated
the place. Add the earthquakes to all this—for the place is
prone to earthquakes, and when it shakes, it's not only
Roumeli that's shaking but the Moreas and the Ionian
islands as well—to give you an idea of what the people have
suffered. As soon as they were rid of one enemy, they would
take courage and set out to rebuild houses and churches
and refortify the town until another enemy fell upon them.
But they never lost faith, and thus, in time, they were able
to consolidate the town of Galaxidi.

When you set foot in the town of Galaxidi today, you immediately sense its decline. And if you happen to be a local who left a long time ago to go to foreign lands, you will remember the greatness that once crowned this devastated place, and you will shed tears guardedly so your fellow countrymen do not notice, those tall old men, hunchbacked after so many years of being tossed about by the sea. They lived during the time when this place was known for its prowess on the sea. They lived (and they still live) during the beautiful time when every one of them was a master on land and sea, and they will in no way admit that times have changed. That is why they will accept your tears as humble greeting of the native soil, and they will be filled with joy because you have not forgotten your homeland.

But if you are a passerby in these parts, and you want to find out how things were long ago, ask which is the church whose bell tower can be seen everywhere you go, from land and sea, mountains and valleys. No matter whom you ask, you will be told in a voice expressing surprise and with a shaking of the head, as if you were asking an improper question, asking about something you should know and, if you did not know, something you should sense from the smell of the sea that reaches the farmland: "St. Nicholas!"

What other saint would have opened his arms with so much goodness as to envelop every mansion and every shack? Just as the shepherd gathers his sheep around him at the onset of bad weather, so St. Nicholas of Galaxidi gathered the town around him, and it settled down on the rocky promontory that separates the two harbors. The one on your left, as you approach from the sea, they named Agora, and the other, on your right, Hirolakka—Widows' Pit. Don't be surprised by this name; it goes back to the time when the Turks occupied the land and fifty newly married women were suddenly attired in mourning black, following a sortie by some young men, all known for their bravery and daring.

From the rocky cape the town slowly spread out to both harbors, like a small child timidly venturing out to play with the waves. Galaxidi today resembles a town of nobles, with its great mansions stooping without losing any of their gentility, the fishing boats mirroring their clear-contoured shapes in the sea, and quite a few caïques that the boatmen work on unhurriedly, as if doing their best to have some of them around as permanent adornment of the dockyard, the only one left in Bistrithra.

In times past, when more people lived here, there were more dockyards and they encircled the town. Wherever there was a harbor, there was also a dockyard; wherever a bay, a place for caïques. At one time Galaxidi had seven thousand souls, they say. Today it has just over two thousand. You can see this for yourself. As you walk along the seashore, you will meet very few people on the way. If you are someone they know, they will keep you company, but if you are a stranger, they will wonder where you came from, they will turn to look at the way you walk, the way you conduct yourself, the way you dress, and if they figure that you are welcome, they will try to approach you and persuade you to visit their home.

But you will have surrendered yourself to the spell of the sea and to the cool breeze that blows down from Liakoura, so why not slip away to Rihi to rest under the trees. You can take the mountain road that leads to the chapel of Sotiras, the Holy Savior. Don't worry about going off course or getting lost. The mountains that surround Galaxidi are rocky and bald. Now and then when they turn green, it's from the sage, the wild vines, the thyme, the holm oak, and the weeds that grow there. If the mountains were green and bushy, the view would be more pleasing to the eye. But now, bare and still as they are, you feel as if there is a brave spirit, stripped of everyday cares, that sits there and studies you as you lay your eyes on them. It does not have the simple, dynastic look of the sea that makes you forget yourself; it does not calm your soul like a stroll in town; nor does it hold the charm of the color green. In this view, if you are strong, you will forget yourself, and you will keep your neighbor at a distance—especially if he happens to be a storyteller, as many a sailor who has seen a great deal is—so you can hold in your hand the soil that burns from the heat of the sun and invigorate both body and soul. Furthermore, you will study carefully the stone loopholes, remnants of 1821; you will think of the battles and the blood that was spilled in this rocky land; and you will be proud if you come from these parts.

But I tell you, you will be dripping with sweat if you attempt to climb up and come down again. So instead, why don't you take the path among the olives, the vineyards, and the almond trees, west of town, climb up to St. Vlasis, and, if you have any stamina left, continue to the chapel of Sotiras. It's not much farther. I swear to you that you will not feel tired because your eyes will be resting constantly on the green of the mountainside, and, when you arrive, you will be in full view of the harbor, the bays, the deserted islets, the sleeping man of Parnassus in the distance, whose hair is snow-covered even in July; a little lower, a peak of the Giona range; and finally, your eyes will rest on the town that will appear in front of you. They have named Sotiras the "balcony of Galaxidi" because nothing interferes with the view. So you can sit like a nobleman and immerse yourself in your reflections. You will just have to say good-day every once in a while to the peddlers from nearby villages who pass by quite often with their wares, or the farmers who are busy weeding, pruning, and watering their fields.

But forgive me for leaving you alone for so long over in Rihi, although at this time, this sweet time in the late afternoon, the women will come to the well to get water for the thirsting oxen and to fill their jugs. But as I go along, I will tell and relate everything to you, one thing at a time, for my memories are many, and they are swarming inside of me like a swarm of bees. May God grant that they become like the sweet water that quenches one's thirst, since they have nourished me and their dew has quenched my thirst ever since I was a child.

First of all, I will relate to you some of the fears and heartaches of the women of Galaxidi in former times. I begin with the women, my reader, because in our place they were the foundation of the family, since the men were always traveling. A good lady of the house can single-handedly secure the nobility of the place, for if the mother walks aright, the whole town follows. My fellow townspeople used to say that every newborn baby girl had her destiny written on her forehead:

> Joy and laughter,
> Tears and sighs.

People used to tell me this when I was a little girl, and I would run to the mirror to see my destiny too. But it was only later, much later, that I realized how true and how deep these words were. And today my thoughts go to my fellow townswomen of long ago, who hid in their bosom a faithful soul, as is shown by the photographs in the heart-shaped frames, decorated with all types of seashells and gold-plated anchors, which their special someone brought as gifts from Marseilles, Livorno, and Genoa. There is still such a picture frame in our house, and on the bottom, in big letters, the following:

FAITH—HOPE—REMEMBRANCE

Grandfather sent it from afar to his special girl, and she saved it until advanced old age.

It was an honor and a duty for a Galaxidi seaman to give his ship—be it a barque, a brig, a barquentine, a schooner, a lugger, or a cutter—the name of his chosen girl before it went out on its first voyage. For this reason, many ships had feminine names, which the rugged men of Galaxidi pronounced with inexpressible sweetness. When the wind puffed up the sails and the ship carved a trail across the sea like a dolphin, the captain, the sailors, the deckhands, all sang the name of the ship. And the captain raised his voice, as if he believed the waves would embrace his song and lay it in the bosom of Galaxidi. And the special someone in the mansion back home would hear her name, and her heart would rejoice.

But even when a squall found them in the open sea or in the midst of so much fog that the captain did not know which way to go, the name of his special lady came to his assistance: "St. Nicholas, save Altana." And the saint would quickly spread his hand over the waves, and the sea would become calm.

On St. Catherine's Day, the ships burst into view one by one. It was the day they returned home. The rugs from Arahova would be spread out in the town's mansions, and decorations brought from foreign parts would be set out: mirrors from Venice, richly trimmed with gold, which took up a whole wall, and you forgot yourself as you looked at them; silver flatware; embroidered bedcovers of fine satin; and finally, a branch of real coral that the captain had bought in Catania. The homes of the captains were not the only ones that were made ready for this occasion. You could see all the ladies freshening up their houses, spreading out their brightly colored rugs and arranging whatever prized objects they had. In terms of silver and gold, I can't say that they matched the well-to-do. But here you enjoyed something else, something extra, that can't be found in the captains' homes, that is to say, seashells of all types, some rounded like bugles, some long and narrow, some open and wide, hundreds of shapes that still had the smell of the sea; sponges, pinnas, and whatever gems of the deep you can think of.

They say that, during the Turkish occupation and the great famine, the town of Galaxidi sold all its adornments and golden items in order to survive. People wondered where all these riches came from—the silk, the embroidered coverlets, the silver items, the flatware. The people of the neighboring villages, who had extra oil and grain, wised up and took advantage of the well-to-do ladies of

Galaxidi, who stooped to the point of giving the most precious thing they had for a mere trifle. And your heart breaks as they tell you how they would come out of their homes as soon as dusk fell and walk in groups during the night so the light of day would not see their impoverishment. In the surrounding villages where they went—I am ashamed to name these villages one by one, as if I am the one to blame—as soon as people saw them, they cried out: "The *kapetanisses* are coming."

Now both the upper and lower floors of the old mansions are bare, but it seems that something remains of the old gentility in the photograph of someone's father in his brig, or of a grandfather's schooner standing proudly in the frame; in a decorative piece made of ebony, a seashell, or a pebble resembling an amulet left on the shelf. But let us leave the present, which makes your heart bleed, and let us return to the town's old gentility.

At the end of the church service, the *kapetanisses,* wearing velvet jackets with gold embroidery, would run to their homes to welcome their captains; and the young women, lowering their eyes, would feel their hearts swelling with longing until the rowboats brought the seafarers to land. But the news traveled ahead of them:

"*Kapetanissa,* good news, the captain is back!" the children would cry out to the wives of the captains.

The feet of the *kapetanissa* would grow wings. She would run to the turn of the narrow road, and as soon as she got a glimpse of her husband coming up the slope, she would return to her home. She would light a candle in front of the *Panayia,* the Holy Mother, and make the sign of the cross. Captain Thimios or Captain Yiannos, any captain, would find her there, in front of the icon. And thus he would remember her when he'd leave, kneeling with tears in her eyes. This is why, when he was in foreign ports, regardless of how many beautiful women he saw, no one came close to the one who prayed silently upon his return and smiled at him when he left. And this is why the seafarer's joy was so great when he stepped on the soil of his homeland. Only, darn it, the road under his feet seemed to give way. He tried to balance his body, but to no avail. The roofs of the houses seemed to be jumping up and down, and the bell towers pitching back and forth. Let them be. In the afternoon, when he went out with the *kapetanissa*, he would lean on her tactfully, and he would walk like a brave young man.

If you are ever in the bay of Galaxidi some spring morning at daybreak, you will see the things I am relating to you revived once again; for as the old mansions wash their shadows in the blue waters and you watch a mirror image of yourself, bent over the gunwale while waiting for the steamer to drop anchor, you will see a grille opening timidly down at the bottom of the sea and a form full of grace and gentility appear. Then your steamer will become a sailing ship, the breeze of your imagination will make the sails swell, and you, young man, will reach out to your beloved.

Only when the steamer heaves anchor, and you are in the open sea, will you say that Galaxidi today is a dead town, without dockyards and without ships; but deep within its bosom remains a shadow, a dream, as it were, of the faithful figure of Penelope.

Translated by Helen Dendrinou Kolias

Lefkas

Ilias Venezis

THE JOURNEY TO LEFKAS is a call, a voice that you hear inside but that you do not hurry to answer. The journey to Lefkas is Sikelianos; it is Valaoritis; it is Madouri; it is the Homeric Ithaca, the passion of Wilhelm Dörpfeld*; it is the legend—it is even the earthquakes. You put off as long as you can the journey to Lefkas. Maybe they tell you it's out of fear of the quakes or the difficult voyage, the difficult road. But you know the secret truth deep inside you is that you are afraid of the encounter with Lefkas, its earth, the water, the air, the mountains, the sea, the olive orchards—everything that poetry has sanctified and made

*The distinguished modern Greek poet Angelos Sikelianos (1884–1951) was a native of Lefkas. The romantic poet Aristotelis Valaoritis (1824–1879), also a native of Lefkas, was a member of a noble family active in the governance of the island and in arranging the terms of its independence from Britain. Madouri, the small island opposite the port of Nydri, is the home of the Valaoritis family. The German archeologist Dörpfeld (1853–1940) believed Lefkas to be the home of Odysseus. [N.B. This and all subsequent notes are provided by the translator.]

spirit and eternity. You are afraid of the difference that separates the one truth from the other, the truth of life from the truth of poetry. Too, you are afraid of the return from the ideal to the reality of Lefkas. What is it, truly, that remains inside you after the excursion to Lefkas: help for the hidden hours in which you are alone and have the need to lean on Lefkas, or Santorini, or Mitikas? Maybe going to the Lefkas of Sikelianos, you will discover the real meaning of Lefkas.

> And seeing all around me, I said:
> "Island
> undiminishing glory in the blue,
> oh rooted
> in the roaring expanse
> and bathed in Homer's verse—
> immersed in the core of the hymn!
> A forest of oak on your peak—
> iron-chorded surge—
> where my entrails seethed in a mist,
> sacred conflagration;
> your edge trembles like a leaf,
> Lefkatas thunders within,
> the rainstorm gathers,
> bursts in the godly olive grove
> stirs up the sea . . .
> Oh my island—
> I will not find anywhere a nurture
>   like my nurturing
> another soul like my soul
> another body like my body."
>   —Angelos Sikelianos

In high youthful tones the poetry of "the Light-shadowed One" sings. Sikelianos is truly there, his soul present, the moment we make out the *kastro*, the fortress of Lefkas.

"Where is the house where Angelos Sikelianos was born?" we ask as soon as we arrive on the island. They guide us to it. It is a modest, well-kept home. The people who live there now maintain it beautifully. It is brilliantly clean, and the wooden floors shine from much polishing. In the room where Sikelianos was born, there is a wooden divan, an old mirror, a trunk, a barometer with the trademark of a tobacco company, a newspaper holder with birds embroidered on it, a framed embroidery spelling "*Kalimera,*" Good Day, and three crosses.

"Who sleeps in this room now?" I ask the young woman of the house, who is serving us sweets.

"I do," she says and blushes. She is called Malakasi, this girl who sleeps in the room where Sikelianos was born.

"Let's go see the churches of Lefkas," says my traveling companion. "After the house of Sikelianos, the churches. That's the way he would have wanted it."

The earthquakes fortunately have not damaged the churches of Lefkas. So we can enjoy the artistry of the white iconostases and the icons of the Doxarades—father and son; of Koutouzis; of Gazis.* Those of us who come from the Aegean part of Greece need an initiation, a spiritual preparation to be able to accept those areas of Orthodoxy influenced by the Italian Renaissance.

*Famous religious artists of the eighteenth century, widely represented in the Ionian islands.

What I find so moving about religious art of the Ionian islands is the conflict, as the spirit of Byzantium is invaded by Western spirituality. This conflict is expressed most often by the hands of anonymous artists and builders who, although they wished to keep their souls pure and the continuity of the Greek tradition inviolable, were caught between two powerful currents.

But how could the icon painters and church builders of Lefkas not have been influenced by the pervasive atmosphere of the Western tradition? They not only lived very close to the sovereignty of Venice but often worked in its service. My companion invited us to pay attention to the character of the faces in the icons of the Doxarades in the church of Ayios Dimitrios. We notice that this Christ does not exhibit the spiritualized form that speaks, through the hand of the naive artist, of the Byzantine tradition. He is portrayed instead as a Venetian aristocrat, and Panayia, the Holy Mother, as an aristocratic Venetian lady.

How could the Ionian Sea ignore Venice? Look at the church of Ayios Minas with its wonderful carved wood iconostasis, with the work of Koutouzis near that of his teacher, Doxaras. Attempting to discover the traditions of the church, we hear about *Galinotati*, the Most Serene One. In 1703, they say, a gigantic plane tree was downed by an earthquake. When the tree fell, an icon was found among its roots. From the *kastro,* the Venetian governor of the island saw, it is said, angels where the tree had stood, and ordered a church to be built there. Thus came about Ayios Minas. How, then, could the iconographer, the carver of the iconostasis, ignore completely the Western style, which made its invasion by means of his patrons?

Similarly, how could the iconographer of the churches of Lefkas not be inspired by the fiery spirit of the seaman, the islander? At the church of Ayioi Anaryiroi, they tell us the following story:

The icon painter Gazis had had it with the church-warden. How could he get revenge on him? He sat down and painted an icon of the Devil with the face of his enemy. What could the churchwarden say? How could he recognize himself in the face of Satan?

The same Gazis raked a certain notable, one Therianos, over the coals as well. This notable had a passion for gaining rights of inheritance to the estates of elderly Lefkadian women who had neither husband nor children. As soon as he learned that a woman was ready to travel to the other world, he would go and butter her up, arranging everything with a notary; hovering between life and death, the woman would deed him her house and belongings. One day, however, on his way to the house of a rich old woman to get her to revise her will, Therianos didn't make it in time. Upon arrival, he found that she had died. Hiding the body, he sought out a poor old wretch named Konstantellos. He dressed the old guy up like an old woman, took him to the house of the deceased, laid him down in the bed, covered him with a sheet, and coached him in what to say to the notary and how to sound like a woman on the brink of death. The notary went to the house and, having determined that the woman Konstantellos was impersonating was of sound mind, began to question her:

"To whom do you leave this house?"

"To Therianos."

"And that house?"

"To Therianos."

"And that other house?"

"To Konstantellos," came the voice from under the sheet.

"Who did you say? Did I hear wrong?" said the astonished Therianos.

"To Konstantellos, I said."

And more softly, "Shut up or I'll show myself, boss."

What could Therianos do? He kept quiet so Konstantellos wouldn't upset the apple cart.

The will was executed, and one of the houses belonging to the departed was inherited by Konstantellos.

Gazis the icon painter wanted to immortalize Therianos the Inheritor. So in the church of Vonitsa, Gazis painted his likeness in the form of a servant of God, angling to inherit the Kingdom of Heaven.

On Lefkas you feel very strongly the bond of the land with the depths, with the spirits of the cosmogony, with the dynamism of the earth. The houses of Lefkas, the churches, the fountains—each human work either prepares itself for earthquakes or, by great cracks and tumbled stones, announces their omnipresence. The new buildings built after an earthquake are not made entirely out of mortar and stone. Joists of wood cross the walls amid the stone and mortar, reminding us that this is a land of fury. Here you see the simple villagers, the women with their firm, erect bodies, rebuilding their houses, calmly preparing for the next quake, which will come sometime. You say, what is human fate? To become accustomed to everything from earthquakes to death, and to find peace precisely in that intimacy with earthquakes and with death.

Here is what is hard to believe: precisely in this land of earthquakes you see the firmest, the proudest, the most upright bodies with heads held high—women's bodies. Until their great old age, the women of Lefkas keep that vertical posture, despite the trembling earth. They learn as children to carry things on their heads, for instance water in little barrels. They put the *podologa,* a coil of cloth, on their heads and settle on it the barrel of water or whatever else they have to carry. And full of joy and dignity, walking with an erect carriage—without the help of their hands, which are spinning wool—they find balance with imperceptible movements of their bodies. This posture, which embodies their attitude toward life and fate, they never lose —as though earthquakes are in their blood. For this reason, the Lefkadian women are among the most beloved in the world. And the most respected mothers.

We found the first "mother of Lefkas" in the famous *kastro* of the island, the Venetian fortress of Santa Maura.*

"What was here, Mother?" All around, the *bidenia,* battlements, are as though cut with a sword. "What was here?" We indicated certain ancient foundations.

This woman, the caretaker of Santa Maura, acting as its deacon, stood among the droppings of animals. The sun had burned her. Around her was the history of her island. "Here was the church of the Pantocrator. Later it became a pig barn. Even later a prison. Now it is as you see it."

In 1938, whatever buildings were left in the *kastro* of

*Santa Maura, *Ayia Maura* in Greek, meaning "Black Saint," was the common name for Lefkas during the Venetian era (1684–1799).

Santa Maura were sold as building materials for ten thousand drachmas. All that remained was the little church.

It seemed the woman thought we had something in our hands; she began to plead with us not to destroy the *kastro* so that what was saved might remain.

"Sir, look at this *kastro* of the Venetians and the Turks! Look at it! That it should be so destroyed, that it should become what you see!"

I looked at her, alone, weak, exquisitely clean, this woman of Lefkas. As though she expressed, in this sunlit hour, all by herself, the nobility of the island and its sorrow; as though she was one with the earth and the sand, the lagoon, the ancestors, and the tears.

Among the droppings was a lone tomb. What were the words chiseled on it? In the sunshine, I bent and saw letters in three languages—English, Italian, and Greek—carved into the stone so they might endure for all eternity: "The General Minister of the Armies of His Britannic Majesty in Sicily. In Memoriam: Enrico Davis."

"He was passing through," the old lady said. "He fell ill here, died, and remained."

The other "mother of Lefkas" we found one day in the village of Vasiliki, on the farm of the good people who were entertaining us. There we experienced the "good old times," the blessings of God, the kindly faces and authentic nobility of our people. It was the time of our fathers. It was the Lefkas of Sikelianos alive and in the flesh, the Lefkas of his "Light-shadowed One" and "Thalero," the youthful one" The elderly lady of Vasiliki, the blessed years showing in the deep lines of her face and her reddened hands, was overseeing everything to do with the table. Around her, her sons, her daughters-in-law, and her grand-children were all looking to her eyes to see what she would command. On the walls were photographs of dead ances-tors, an indispensable decoration on Lefkas.

"Maybe we didn't eat meat on Sundays," said the elderly lady. "However, if something was to us a matter of pride, we would do it. That's why we have the photographs." And a little later: "Soon my children will have a photograph taken of me, so they will remember me with pride."

The table was princely. Only the men sat around it, while, standing, the women of the house attended the guests with slow, soft movements. The old lady, seated on the *fortseri*, the trunk, reigned authoritatively, telling the daughters-in-law to fill our glasses with *robola*, the local wine, and to bring us food.

At the proper time, the elderly woman began to recite "Thalero." Caught up in the Dionysian time that encom-passed us all, out of the power of solid things, out of the poetry of life, of beauty, of joy, of wine, and of death, with her warm voice she brought among us the living Sikelianos, the great master of Lefkas and the Ionian islands. Never have I felt so close to him, to his very breath, as there in the farm in Vasiliki on the shore of Lefkas:

> And at the house ahead, beneath the unripe vine,
>> a ready table
> waited for me, a lamp hung out in front of it—
>> the evening star.
> There the master's daughter brought me
>> honeycomb, cold water, country bread;

her strength had engraved around her rocklike
    throat a circle like a dove's ring:
. . . .
There the old wine was opened for me,
    smelling rich in the porous jar,
as mountain scents when the cool night dew
    falls on the bushes.

Glowing, festive, warm, there my heart
    consented to repose for a while
in sheets made fragrant by herbs, azure
    by washing blue.

                —Angelos Sikelianos

               Translated by Alison Cadbury

Sioulas the Tanner

Dimitris Hatzis

Deep and blue-green, the lake spreads out beside the small town. In its waters are reflected the high walls of the old medieval castle, which some say goes even further back.

Just outside the eastern wall of the castle, right on the edge of the lake, were the tanneries. The tanners who lived in this quarter were known as *tabaki*, a similar name being used at Serres, Voloś, and, I believe, on Syra.

The animal hides used to be stretched tightly on wooden frames in the lake water along the whole length of the quarter. When quite soaked the hides would be taken and tanned in the workshops.

In all, there were some fifteen to twenty of these workshops or tanneries, in a row beneath the castle wall. Each one was two-storied, built of stone, and had a large arched doorway. The ground floor had small windows like loopholes and consisted solely of a broad stone-paved entrance hall, wooden washtubs lying about here and there. In these halls, either barefooted or shod in a kind of large boot, stripped to the waist and trouserless, the tanners worked on the hides. The upper floor jutted out half a meter above the road and had large Venetian-style windows. Here were the living quarters, reached by a small wooden staircase from within the workshop. The whole district stank with the pungent reek of animal skins.

The tanners boasted descent from the town's earliest inhabitants, as well as from the leading families who had lived within the castle until ejected by the Turks after the Skylosophos uprising in 1612. And indeed, they spoke the town dialect in a purer form than anyone else, keeping it intact both in vocabulary and pronunciation.

They scarcely ever went up into the town except on special business and, in fact, had very little to do with it. They were disdainful of newcomers and it's highly likely that they had no idea even of the neighborhoods where the refugees from Asia Minor had made their homes. The tanners lived in their own isolated, self-sufficient world, beyond the castle walls.

At no distance at all from their workshops stood the woodyards where Vlachs from Metsovo and the Zagoria worked. The tanners had absolutely nothing to do with them. And a couple of roads further up were the coopers—Metsovite Vlachs, too, with others from the villages of Vovousa and Dobrinovo. For years these men had pounded away with their wooden mallets at the wild pine and beech they used for their barrels. Yet here again the tanners kept to themselves, for though they knew these men well enough to bid them good morning, and had no quarrel with them, this was as far as it went. After all, such people were mere carrot-crunchers, *datskanaraii*—uncouth villagers.

At the front the workshops looked toward the *Skala*, or Steps, as the landing-stage was called. It was here that the large lake-going caïques, slow-moving skiffs, unloaded goods such as firewood, slaughtered livestock, cheeses, and butter from the villages opposite. But the tanners only bought things there when it was necessary; otherwise they kept to themselves for, once again, what had they in common with villagers? In the evenings they went to their own wineshops where no villager ever set foot except for the boatmen from the small island in the lake. These would sometimes have a drink or two with the tanners before going back home for the night. It was only because the two groups shared a passion for hunting that the tanners let them join them.

During the winter, braziers would be placed in special holes in the low tables in these drinking dens and the tanners would sit round on stools that were low, too, warming their wine in copper pots before drinking it. The conversation always revolved upon past episodes, hunting and the like. Hard and proud men, they rarely brought work or such matters into the talk—they thought it beneath them to do so. Nor did they discuss politics, for all were of one mind, being staunch Venizelists: the greater "Greece of the Five Seas," as befitted descendants of castle notables. They always voted for the Venizelist mayor and the Venizelist councillers of the Cathedral of St. Athanasios. And here the matter ended, for they were totally self-sufficient in their moral, social, and political outlook.

And in professional matters, too, for their trade guild, according to those qualified in such knowledge, was one of the oldest in the town, and had remained unchanged over the passage of time. Tanners neither left the guild nor did newcomers enter it. The only difference was that during the years I'm writing about, since the remaining tanners were all interrelated, they reorganized their workshops into partnerships. There was no distinction between head workman and apprentice—everyone was a head workman and a steady respectable citizen at the same time. But it was only in this instance that the guild tradition had altered. In every other way it continued to function as it had always done since its inception in those distant days when the tanneries were first established. The tanners took no interest in how their trade was carried on elsewhere. They came by their dyestuffs from local natural sources, and used them in ways traditionally imparted to them. Even their glue— *toukali,* as it was known—was obtained from the fish in the lake. Indeed, everything they used was acquired in a similar manner and employed according to practices handed down from generation to generation.

And it was by family tradition that Sioulas had become a tanner, for he was the son of a tanner and his wife was the daughter of one. He'd grown up among the tanneries and played the games of childhood there: knuckle-bones and *sklentza,* as they called tip-cat, and quoits, leapfrog and prisoner's base. He'd taken part in the stone-throwing fights with the children from the nearby neighborhoods. There, too, he'd learned to read and write, and had first attended church and gone hunting on the lake. Then eventually he'd entered the tanning trade, married, and founded his own family. And all the time he was possessed of an ingrown pride. Steadfastly moderate in everything, he saw any kind of innovation as blatant showing off.

A relative of his had gone to live abroad for a while: an extremely rare occurrence. And then suddenly he was back again, complete with gold watch-chain on his waistcoat and flaunting his money. Blood being thicker than water, he kept to his own kind and roamed around the tanneries by day and sat in the tanners' wineshops by night. All quite natural, yet what irked his companions was the way he would all at once hold forth about his experiences abroad, never able to suppress the desire to regale them with tales of the wonderful things he had seen. At first they looked at him angrily; then they spoke sharply to him a few times. But it was of no avail.

One midday in the summertime the tanners, as usual nearly naked when they'd been working, came out of their workshops for a break and to give the food they'd just eaten a chance to settle. Our traveler was there and on the point of launching into one of his stories.

"I wonder if you could tell us," began Sioulas suddenly, slowly rising and going over to him, "did you learn anything of those foreign languages while you were away there in Europe?"

"Yes, sure, a bit," answered our unsuspecting friend.

"Right, then, perhaps you'd like to tell us what it says here." So saying, Sioulas turned his back on him and slapped the label on his underpants.

The tanners roared with laughter, as did their wives at their windows.

Sioulas kept angrily slapping his backside:

"Come on, mate, read it out!"

From that day the man was never again seen wearing his

watch-chain or speaking of his travels or money—certainly not in the presence of the tanners. There was no more trifling with them.

Meanwhile time passed, everyone gradually aged, and year by year the castle walls slowly crumbled. But people were too preoccupied to notice the changes going on around them. Sioulas's hair began to turn white without his realizing it. The evening would often find him with his legs stiff from the long years they'd been immersed in water when he was working. Every year Sioulaina, just like a rabbit, would produce a new little Siouling, and a tribe of children has to be fed, clothed, shod, and sent to school. When you're in that situation, ground down by daily worries, there's no time to look around and take stock of things.

All the tanners, in fact, were too harassed to take much account of what was happening around them, of how and when the changes in their trade—now steadily worsening —had started. Materials and goods, cheaper and better produced, had begun to be brought in from elsewhere: kidleather, patent-leather, shoes, raincoats, even calf-hide and the leather for soles. A few of the older leather businesses in the town's bazaar now found it more profitable to obtain their raw hides and send them directly to Italy, Marseilles, and even Syria for machine-processing, rather than troubling with the tanners.

An atmosphere of gloom began to settle over the oppressed tanners every evening in their wineshops. A number of them only worked two or three days a week now. There were those burdened with the knowledge that there was no food in their homes for the evening meal. And everyone knew that their womenfolk begged from one another, sharing their misfortune among themselves, though they would not admit this to their husbands and each sought to conceal the tanner's plight within his own household when he had no work.

The men themselves never complained about their poverty, nor revealed signs of it. They would certainly have been ashamed to do so before one another. Nor would they have dreamed of finding other work outside the tanneries —it would have seemed an act of treachery. They all rallied to the defense of their besieged profession. And in the town every Sunday morning during the winter their double-barreled shotguns could be heard resounding from the lake, like a mighty witness to their noble and manly passion for hunting.

At the great shoots on the lake when the birds would be steadily enclosed—a big event in which everyone took part along with the regular hunters—the tanners excelled themselves. It had been established as a sort of right that they would start out from the farthest end of the lake before dawn, rowing softly, driving the frightened flocks of waterfowl toward the center of the lake by firing their guns. There were *yesia* and *kanaves*—as the male and female wild duck were called—and black coots with white bills. And sometimes there were the large beautiful wild geese whose soft fleecy underwing, below their breasts, and known as *balsamo*, is kept by the womenfolk as ideal for treating wounds.

With their shotguns ready, the other hunters from the town and island would be standing in their small boats, which were lined up in the middle of the lake. Since the birds would fall upon them in the hundreds, all that was required was one pair of hands to keep firing a gun and another to load it—a job usually done by the boatman, who would also ease his boat over the water to gather the birds in. Each bird was accounted as belonging to the boat it had fallen nearest, regardless of who had actually shot it.

On these great lake shoots, or on his own solitary Sunday hunting expeditions, Sioulas would relive the sorrows and longings of his proud soul from the days of his youth to the beginnings of old age, when life had taken such a turn for the worse, reducing him to poverty. Now in the evenings he would return home in a state of exhaustion, his legs stiff from sitting all day in the narrow boat and his clothes sodden. He would back into the doorway, shoulder the door open and drop his catch in the middle of the room, and then stretch out face downward beside the hearth, on the place called the *bassi* that all houses had in their winter room. He would get his children to tread up and down his aching back, which they would do with yells and shouts of laughter, giving him delighted kicks. He would shout out with them, while the dog went wild, not knowing whom to bark at first. It was one moment of happiness amid the general cloud of darkness that had engulfed the tanneries.

But at the same time Sioulaina would be kneeling on the floor counting and recounting the birds: four for themselves, a pair for her sister, a pair for her mother-in-law. And the rest? What if they sold the rest? This was a thought she dare not reveal to him even by the look in her eyes. The boatmen, the islanders, and the other poor men of the town would go hunting and enjoy themselves, eat what they wanted of their catch and then sell the rest in the bazaar—they on their own or their women and children. But a tanner—never. Not for the whole world.

There came a time when Sioulas's workshop stood idle all week. Nor was there any proper work at the other workshops. His wife only managed to cope by scouring the house for what scraps of food there were, seeking help from the other women, and, in fact, by secretly selling things to the Jewish rag-and-bone man who had got wind of what was happening in the tanneries. Sioulaina didn't speak to her husband all that week; she asked for nothing from him, she didn't even look him in the eyes. But now she could take no more. She sat crying with her head in her arms, waiting for the others to come in for their midday meal— only to find she had nothing for them.

He made his way up, entered the room, saw her sitting in a corner and felt his children's eyes fixed upon him.

"What do you mean by letting the children go hungry like this?"

She didn't speak. She sat in the corner with her head bowed.

"Didn't you try to get anything from the grocer's?"

She raised her eyes and looked at him, without sorrow, complaint, or anger, just an unspoken plea to him not to go on. But he grew more angry.

"Why don't you say something for goodness' sake? What's the matter with you?"

She lowered her face again.

"He won't let us have anything more." She said it humbly, as if she were to blame.

"And what about bread? How come you didn't get any?"

"The baker won't let us have anything, either."

She got up and hurried out to hide the choking tears—tears at his unfairness rather than the misfortune that had befallen them.

The children fled, she followed, going to her sister to seek mutual solace. He stayed in the room, alone in the empty house all afternoon, not thinking about their plight nor of his wounded pride and his shame before his children but about his wife, about his injustice to her. He kept catching back a sob—this was the first time in their twenty married years that he had ever seriously thought about her.

It was beginning to get dark when he rose. None of the others had returned home yet. He took down the shotgun and looked at it carefully several times before putting it under his arm and going down out of the house.

"What's the problem?" asked the Gypsy, about to take the gun.

He had no appetite for small talk. The fellow was in every way a Gypsy, a back-street gunsmith who repaired poor men's guns for next to nothing in a mean hole in the *bizestenia* next to the bellmakers' workshops. Sioulas kept hold of the gun, staring at the other keenly.

"I'm selling it," he said briefly, finally handing him the gun. "I'm getting another one."

It was a fine Belgian double-barreled, twelve-bore, without hammers. The Gypsy knew it of old and left it in the tanner's hands, without even looking at it. He regarded him, the dark mischievous eyes playing in the swarthy face.

"No, don't do that, Sioulas, old pal."

"What, you'll not take it?"

"Sure, I'd take it all right, and make a fair bit on it."

"Come on, no Gypsy tricks, I'm not going to haggle. What'll you pay?"

"I know you won't get another one," said the other calmly, used to being called "Gypsy" and not troubled by it. "You've got problems. No work. There's your kids. But don't sell the gun, old pal, you'll never see it again."

The Gypsy wasn't bargaining.

"I know what it's like. There's been other tanners here, things are rough. But when they've only had the one gun I've not taken it. For years I've made my living from poor blokes like you, so give it to someone else. I'm not dirtying my hands doing a thing like that."

Sioulas stared at the ground. A Gypsy had called him a poor bloke, and wouldn't dirty his hands with his—Sioulas's —gun. But it was not because of these things—he was not even thinking about them. It was something else: for the second time the same day he found himself thinking about his unjust behavior. "Why didn't you get some bread from the baker's?" "No Gypsy tricks with me!" If the Gypsy had-n't at that moment taken out his tobacco for them both to roll cigarettes he would have left quickly, quite ashamed.

"Yes, you're right," he said, after a moment or two, with-out raising his eyes. And then he did raise them, and looked at him. "You're a good man." He said it smiling, as if it were the Gypsy's just due. He made to go.

The Gypsy stopped him.

"I know what it's like," he repeated. "You've difficulties, no work, the children. But don't let your gun go; you're a tanner, you'll not get over it."

He took out a hundred-drachma note and gave it to him.

"Pay it back when you can."

Sioulas took it: took it and felt no shame. He clutched it in his fist and as he did so began to feel a tender euphoria seep right through him, body and soul, like a new warmth. And it wasn't because he'd have some money to take home. It was because for the first time in his life he had felt close to other people, to poor people, as he himself had been called by the Gypsy; because he felt an understanding of himself: you aren't an unjust man, Sioulas. As he made his way through the streets back down to the tanneries he felt this new warm living thing astir within him, glowing there. Something almost like joy at the heart of the black despair, something that could never die.

Night had fallen by the time he walked past the wood-men's and coopers' yards. He heard someone calling him. It was a round, ruddy-faced cooper from Metsovo with a back misshapen from perpetual bending over work.

"Good evening."

"Where are you going with your gun at this time of day?"

"Oh, it needed straightening a bit, I've just taken it to the Gypsy. He's a good man," he said unexpectedly, without meaning to.

"Don't know him," said the cooper. "Still, he hasn't done anything to us, has he? Come and have a *raki*."

He had never been in this wineshop before—it was a khan and wineshop combined where woodyard men, coopers, respectable family men, poor men of the neighborhood, and villagers staying the night in town went. The cooper bought him a *raki* and started talking about the lack of work and great difficulties.

"You people aren't in too good a shape, either," he said at one point.

"No," replied Sioulas. He didn't feel at all ashamed at saying this. "We're certainly not."

"So what will you do?"

"No idea. No one has."

"It's a lousy business," added the cooper.

He wasn't listening to him anymore. At that moment he was aware of something overflowing within him, prompting him to do nothing but get up and buy everyone in there a drink: Vlachs, Gypsies, villagers, poor men, every single one of them. But it remained an impulse, and after treating the cooper to a return *raki* he bade him a cheerful good-night.

"He's a good man, too," he thought and kept repeating it to himself to get the full flavor and meaning of it. "But where the hell have they all been hiding?"

Entering the street where the tanneries stood he came upon one of his own youngsters. He called him and surreptitiously slipped him some money to give to his mother, and handed over the gun as well. He felt too self-conscious to go up himself at that moment and only came back late at night when he could be sure she would be in bed asleep. He lay beside her on the mattress and neither of them spoke or stirred all night.

Before dawn he rose and tiptoed down with his gun, his wife still not stirring. He got in the little boat and headed for the open lake, to the part known as the Great Deep. He thrust his oars deep into the water, hurriedly rowing through the reedbeds.

By the time he returned home a cold bright winter's day had already fully dawned. He stood outside the door of his workshop and shouted. His children came down and stared awestruck at the rich game. He unslung the gun from his shoulder and handed it to them, along with three ducks.

"Give them to your mother" was all he said.

He set off again, taking about ten of the birds with him, without glancing back at the house where he knew, behind the windowpane, her eyes were full of tears. He made his way right through the tanneries, past the workshops, to the bazaar, his head high and his steps ringing out.

And that's how the first tanner took his game to sell in the bazaar. The others followed. The trumpets announcing a new dawn that day toppled the tanners' Jericho to its very foundations amid the deafening roar of machinery. Spring was drawing near and flocks of wild geese began flying ever higher above the lake. It was as if they, too, had taken fright.

Translated by David Vere

Carnival

Christoforos Milionis

Far away, in
another world
this carnival took place
　　　　　— M. Sahtouris

THAT WINTER was the hardest.

Winter is always hard in Yiannena,* with the frost descending from the Pindos Range, the north winds sweeping away the empty nests of the storks from the rooftops, the rain pounding night and day on the gutter next door, the same tempo for months on end, and the sky so low and sullen it seems you will never again see the face of the sun. That is why I say that those who explain allegorically the familiar verses

> everywhere clear skies, everywhere sun,
> but in poor Yiannena dark rain and fog

as if they have to do with *sklavia***—even though *sklavia*

---

*"Yiannena" is the colloquial name of Ioannina.
***Sklavia* implies the subjugation of a people and the occupation of their land. *Trans.*

was never absent from this place—apparently do not know this city very well.

However, that winter we were literally in the throes of death. The Civil War was seething in the countryside, and the hordes of refugees from Pogonia and Konitsa and from as far away as Zagorohoria, Tsamouria, and Laka-Souli had descended on the town. We arrived with an army convoy, villagers and soldiers piled in the back of the army truck. The minesweepers went in front, and every so often they would get down and search the road with their electrical brooms inch by inch, so the sixty kilometers became an endless journey. The women threw up, then they complained that they were cold and the soldiers pulled down the canvas. We were confined to stench and silence. Later on a villager started talking with the soldiers about his family, and then they turned the conversation to the four Gypsies who were with us.—Where in the devil were they off to with their instruments at such a time when everything was going up in smoke?—The villager related the following incident:

Not long ago a Gypsy set off on his donkey to go to Zagorohoria to trade. On the way, he comes upon a group of men.

"Where are you from?" they ask him.

"From the villages in the plain."

"What's your name?"

"Fezo—Fezo and also Yiannis." His old name was Fezo; his new name is Yiannis.

"Why did you have yourself baptized?"

"That's what they told us to do."

"And why don't you tell us," they ask him, "whose side you're on?"

The Gypsy looks at the hats for a crown—he sees neither crown nor letters. "On your side," he says.

"Whose?"

"Yours." He said nothing else, so they had him stand six meters away—and that was the end of it for him.

The soldiers laughed: "And so, Grandpa, neither party found out which side the other was on."

Then one of the soldiers turned and asked the villager who had told the story: "If you were in his shoes, what would you say?"

At first he shrank back, but suddenly his face lit up and he said, "I would take a gamble: *korona—grammata.*"*

But the soldier wanted to play with it a little longer, and he turned to one of the Gypsies, an old man with a drooping mustache and grimy cap, and said: "Really, old man, you Gypsies, whose side are you on?"

The old Gypsy smiled cunningly, tilted his head to the side, and said in as wretched a manner as he could muster: "Your side." Villagers and soldiers laughed loudly. "Then," the soldier said, "play the national anthem for us."

The Gypsies looked at one another. "We shouldn't," the old man said, "the big guy will be angry with us."

The soldier insisted, and the Gypsies took their instruments out of their pouches and began to play the old march

---

*Korona—grammata (literally, "crown—letters") is the equivalent of the English expression "heads or tails." However, because the word *korona* (crown) is associated with the king, and thus with the royalists, and the word *grammata* is associated with abbreviated forms of leftist groups, the Greek expression lends itself easily to political wordplay. *Trans.*

for the king, "The Son of the Eagle,"* as they sat on baskets and bundles of clothing, among women who had vomited and held their white scarves tightly over their mouths. The convoy stopped again. Someone approached the truck and shouted: "Shut up, for Christ's sake. Is this a time for celebration?" The instruments stopped sounding, the Gypsies mumbled something among themselves with an expression that indicated, "The man is right," and a soldier raised the back canvas of the truck. A rush of cool air and dampness entered, stirring up the stench of gasoline and vomit. Darkness had fallen, and it was raining. Someone said, "The minesweeper is out in front," and everyone fell silent again. And the truck started rolling and stopping again and again in deadly silence. When we arrived in Yiannena, midnight was approaching, and it was raining heavily.

We walked from inn to inn, sticking to covered sidewalks, but in our hurry we often walked past open gutters and were drenched by all the rainwater that we had previously managed to avoid. We could not find a place to stay. Everywhere we ran into throngs of refugees trying to poke their heads in the innkeepers' windows and pleading for a room, or at least for a covered corner adjoining the house, where they could spread out a heavy *velentza*, for they had

---

*The soldier asked the Gypsies to play the national anthem (the "Hymn to Liberty"), but they mistook the order and instead played the march for the king. The substitutions show the confusion of meanings during that troubled period of the Civil War (cf. Thucydides, *History* 3.82.4).

young children and they would catch pneumonia. And all around the women were waiting patiently, holding crying babies in their arms and sitting on their belongings. No one even thought of going to a good hotel, penniless as we were; besides, in these too, they said, there was not even an empty hallway to be found anywhere. Finally, we made do in the "Family Inn," where the innkeeper—a heavy old man who moved about in unbuttoned pajamas all day, his belly hanging out and his slippers dragging on the tiles—let us sleep on the floor for pay, in the same room where he himself slept with his old lady. Nights were difficult, with the floorboards rubbing your bones, the old lady snoring, her chin hanging down and her yellowish strands of hair spread all over the pillow, and the old man coughing and farting. We tried to be patient (this was a temporary setup), and during the day we searched from morning till evening in hopes of finding something better. Those who had been the first to arrive had managed to get the Jewish homes of the Kastro, which had been empty for four years now and were falling into ruin. Even the schools that had been built thanks to the bequests of native sons, the Zosimades and the Kaplanides, were full. So a committee was formed and began to make requisitions. Understandably, the people of Yiannena who had been branded as collaborators during the time of the Nazi occupation let them requisition one, even two rooms without any objections. Often they themselves huddled willingly in one room, giving up the rest of their house. —"We would not leave the people on the street," they used to say, charitably and hesitatingly so their words would not be misunderstood. The problem was with the others, who had raised their nose high in the air; they were not afraid, for they always knew someone in the garrison headquarters or in the governor's office who would cancel the requisition for them. Because in such situations things could get very mixed up, the Committee withdrew whenever it met with insistent objections. However, as things became tighter, it started taking harsher measures.

So the Committee of Refugee Housing—that was its official name—first sent us to the home of the banker R. I still remember the hesitation with which we opened the iron garden gate and proceeded among beds of chrysanthemums that stirred gently under the light rain. There were verandas with climbing vines, columns in the front of the house, and a crystal door. We pressed the doorbell very respectfully and waited. Someone was playing the piano inside. Finally, the wife of the banker, a woman with light blue hair who was wearing a crimson robe, came out and showered us with abuses. They had already requisitioned one of her rooms, and since then, she said, she did not have control of her bath, she did not have control of her privy. I did not know what this last thing meant, and it took me a long time to find out. For many years it wandered in my imagination, wrapped in the melody of the piano, like a chocolate in gold foil, which fascinated me just as much. We mentioned these things to the Committee, and they sent her a family from the Vlach villages together with a trooper who forced the door with a metal rod and installed them inside. It was at the direct order of the garrison leader, they said, who had been angered by what was happening.

As for us, we were finally housed in a room belonging to Kyr Yiannis Pliatsikas, who was a grave digger in Perivlefti, we soon found out. Of course, we did not like his unusual vocation, for it was like sleeping side by side with Death, but this was no time for luxuries. We had to deal with something worse: the room, a space set apart from the rest of the house and probably intended for storage, had a wooden wall and no windows, only a skylight high in the ceiling, through which entered only the noise of the rain and the wind but not a drop of light. We had to have the electric light on even during the day. In the beginning the grave digger had objections also: "I have a girl and you have a boy; I don't want any headaches," he said and looked at me. Skinny and undernourished as I was, coming out of a childhood spent under the occupation, it had not occurred to me that perhaps I had grown up. However, when the Committee person who accompanied us (and, as a resident of Yiannena, apparently was familiar with people and events) told him that he already had enough headaches and it was impossible that he could acquire greater ones, the old man lowered his head and said, "Okay." In the beginning we assumed it had to do with his daughter, a heavy-set girl with hair resembling that of Genovefa,* which reached down to her buttocks. Some rumor about her must have been going around. However, all that winter we stayed there, she never left the laundry room and the kitchen. Anyway, in time this matter was forgotten, and the grave digger slowly became more friendly and even let us cook in his kitchen, using the oil burner, and gave us a tin brazier for charcoal. We also got used to him—to him and to his work.

There was nothing unusual about him to speak of. He

---

*A legendary heroine (her name is a variant of Genevieve), once popular in Greece, commonly depicted with long hair to cover her naked body.

used to come home with his shoes and hands full of mud, as if he were returning from working in the melon field; he washed the dirt off his hands at the tin-covered shed, said good evening to the women in the kitchen, and came in to change. Timidly in the beginning, but more often later on, he took courage and started coming to our room in the evening to keep us company for about an hour. Toward the end, he used to bring even his bottle of *raki* to treat us. His swollen eyes then became red and shined on his broad face, which had a childlike innocence, even though it was always unshaven. "You drink too much, Kyr Yianni, and it's not good for you. It will harm you," we used to tell him. "Can't get through this winter otherwise, with death over your head," he answered in a hoarse voice that came from his seething chest, and he reached for the bottle, his hand full of calluses from digging and shoveling. "Everything came all at once," he added.

Naturally, we also talked about the state of affairs, obviously not about politics, which for most people had been reduced to the formula *bourantades—katsapliades*,* but about more tangible things: What would they distribute to the refugees? When would we return to our homes? But certainly, even these everyday concerns were tied to other actions, and in some way to politics. "Don't believe anything," Kyr Yiannis said; "it's all propaganda. I, Kyr Yiannis Pliatsikas, am telling you, and you will remember that I told you so." And then he told us another version, totally different from the one we had heard on the street from the swarms of refugees. We could tell that he had just come

---

*These are colloquial terms referring to the government troops and to the guerrilla troops. *Trans.*

away from listening to the radio: at this time of day, always at the same hour, its voice penetrated the thin wall of our room, and we understood that it transmitted the "Voice of Truth,"* but we did not say anything. And when the big battles started in Konitsa and the airplanes were flying low overhead and sweeping the city every second, he used to come home flushed, and without stopping at the usual place to wash off, say a curt good evening to the women, and bolt the door behind him. In a little while he would come out holding his bottle: "It's all propaganda, don't believe anything. They're holding on to Konitsa, and they'll make it the capital." And one time in his excitement, brought on by the *raki,* he said angrily, "It will become the grave of the *bourantades.*" Only when the planes stopped coming and going and the Fix Prison was full and there were parades in the center of town did he become bitter and stop talking. Then came the court-martial, and with a single decision forty-eight were condemned to death. At dawn we would hear the army truck, which passed by at the same time every morning, taking them to the quarries, a few at a time. People became very cold to one another. Kyr Yiannis stopped receiving outlawed stations, and he made his visits less frequent until he finally stopped visiting altogether. In fact, he had an air about him, as if he considered us responsible for all this. And when we happened to run into one another at the door and we asked him matter-of-factly, "How are things, Kyr Yianni?" he would answer hurriedly, "Fine, fine." Only once did he try to smile: "Thank God, as long as we are well, and death too."

*A Communist radio station broadcast by a neighboring country.

Amid all of that, we managed in that setup, and what was meant to be temporary became permanent. Others were worse off. Those who had not managed to find housing in private homes lived in wooden shanties pierced by the cold, former landlords and recent prostitutes mixed together. Anyway, winter was held at bay, even though that winter was the hardest.

Around Carnival time, the weather improved. It was still cold, of course, and often it turned to frost, but the endless rains subsided, and people began to pour out to the center of town in the evening and to stroll up and down excitedly. And the soldiers began to follow the refugee girls as they walked together arm in arm; or to stare at the photographs of Deanna Durbin and Maria Montez in front of the movie theaters and to listen to the songs of Stella Greca coming from the loudspeaker:

> *the short little waltz*
> *echoing in the clock.*

At ten *Thodora* passed by—three buglers, that is, who called them to quarters—and the soldiers broke away in groups from the taverns—the "Garden of Allah," the "Five F's,"*and "Alexi's" place—and headed for the Akraios and the Kastro army barracks, singing *rembetika* songs with their arms entwined and their berets stuck under their shoulder straps, daring the military police as they passed by:

---

*The name "The Five F's" stands for five Greek words, all of which begin with F, that mean: "Friend, Bring Friends, Eat, Leave."

some day they will find me
lying in the middle of the street.

And the people dispersed from the square.

The evening of *Apokria*,* there was a lot of merrymaking. Booths with paper hats, ribbons, and confetti had been set up on the sidewalks of the square, and the young men had adorned every girl with multicolored butterflies, even some sickly refugee girls from beyond Souli who wore the native black dress of their district. Near midnight the strollers, worn out, headed for their homes. Then a few groups of people came out of the nearby taverns, boys and girls together, wearing paper hats and false noses; singing out of tune, they began to dance the samba in the middle of the square. A crowd gathered around them, and, hesitatingly at first, later less so, they formed couples and joined in the dance. The merriment flared up when two cornet players came forth and coordinated the rhythm, and thus, within a short while, the whole square had become a huge dance floor. Most people, of course, did not know how to dance the samba, which had only recently become popular, but with awkward movements they tried to imitate those who seemed to know it.

Suddenly there was a great disturbance. People started leaving the dance and running toward the garrison head-quarters, where they asked questions of those who had arrived before them or stood on tiptoes trying to see what was going on. The cornet players stopped and the dance broke up. The gathered crowd made way for a couple of

*Sunday of Carnival.

revelers, two soldiers on an unsaddled donkey, which was
bowed down in the middle and staggering under the
weight. The men were holding a bottle each and were
singing hoarsely (dead drunk as they were) and shaking
their dragging feet comically. Behind them, a swarm of
devilish children poked the donkey with sticks and made a
lot of noise. The procession stopped in front of the garrison headquarters, and the two riders struck the animal to
goad it through the gate, where the guard had raised his
hands in exasperation and was trying to stop them. The
unfortunate animal, which could move neither forward nor
backward, suddenly let out a desperate bray that echoed
through the square, like taps when the flag is lowered. At
the same time it twisted its rump, as the two soldiers tried
to balance themselves on its back while yelling angrily at
the guard: "Make way, office boy." The garrison chief
appeared on the balcony, along with officers of his staff, and
one officer ran down the steps on the outside of the building. The riders dismounted and, holding the scruff of the
donkey, one on the right and the other on the left, managed to stand at attention and to salute. They tried to be
formal, but everything beyond "I have the honor, General,
Sir," was drowned out by the shouts of the crowd. A soldier pulled the animal away and, hitting it on the backside
with the palm of his hand, led it behind the building. The
two drunken men followed the officer up the steps and,
before entering the building, stopped for a moment and
waved triumphantly to the applauding and cheering crowd.
Suddenly one of them stuck his hand in the sack he was
carrying on his back and lifted a human head up high,
holding it by its long hair. The people below froze, and the
uproar came to an abrupt end. When the door opened both

officers and soldiers disappeared inside, and the garrison chief with his staff withdrew as well and closed the balcony door behind them, pulling the crimson drapes shut.

Word spread that the two drunks were a private and a corporal who had set an ambush the previous night. A group of guerrillas had gone to set mines on the road, and the two sides exchanged fire. The other guerrillas managed to get away in the darkness. Only their leader was left; he lay on the ridge crying out that he was giving up and that they should come take him because he was hit. The corporal said to stop firing; he took the private with him, and, moving this way and that, they approached the place where they had heard the voice. A burst of gunfire from an automatic was discharged over their heads. They barely managed to get down in time, and the corporal threw a grenade. "The creep," he said, "he almost killed us." He took the guy's head to bring it himself to the headquarters. Arriving in the city in the morning, he and his companion made themselves at home in the first tavern they came across and stayed there until evening. They even turned on the music and danced. Later on they found the donkey and bet they could enter the garrison headquarters riding, knowing that the military police would look the other way, since the police were comfortably in the safety of the city, they did not dare to argue with those who were constantly risking their lives. This is what people were saying in the square as the crowd dispersed. But others said nothing. They just wandered off with their heads bent down.

That same night, near dawn, we heard loud knocking on our landlord's front door. Then, the creaking of the bed on the other side of the thin wall, a quiet exchange of words, and again more knocking. "Just a minute, just a minute," Kyr Yiannis called out and, dragging his feet, went to open up. "The headquarters," he said when he came back. "They want me to go." And his voice was trembling. Again whispers were heard, this time with sobs, and finally the door closed and it was quiet again. It was still dark—it wouldn't be right for us to get up and ask questions and make noise at such an hour. Everyone had his concerns; let us pretend that we heard nothing, and when day comes we will see. And we went back to sleep.

But when day came, no one appeared, either in the laundry room or in the kitchen. The house was quiet all day, so much so that we assumed the owners were away, that perhaps they had gone to be with relatives for *Kathari Deftera,* the beginning of Lent. Not until evening did we hear something from the corner room, something like quiet crying, like drowned moaning, but it was not possible, we must have made a mistake, or perhaps the mice that often played tag in the cornices and under the old floorboards had found an opportunity, now that the owners were gone, and were breeding undisturbed in the rooms.

On Tuesday, around noon, I ran into a neighbor who was standing on her tiptoes trying to see inside the window of our building that faces the street. I asked her whom she was looking for. "Didn't you notice anything," she whispered, "or are you pretending that you know nothing?" I told her that we knew nothing. Then she came closer and said, "Yesterday at daybreak they called the old man to identify the head of his son, who was a guerrilla, a captain, and was killed the eve of *Apokria.* They gave it to him to bury, so no one would find out." And she ended by launching into a monologue: "They're poor people, why did they get mixed up in politics?"

The next day the owners appeared at their usual occupations: the woman in the kitchen, the girl in the laundry room, and Kyr Yiannis leaving for work, his head lowered. This time they did not even open their mouth to respond to our "good morning." Their eyes were red, and we pretended we did not notice. We just looked to find a shanty covered with tar paper and moved there after a few days. At least temporarily. Besides, the brunt of winter had passed, and we hoped that something would be done by the following year.

Translated by Helen Dendrinou Kolias

Angel John the Thief

Georgios Drosinis

A ROBBERY HAD TAKEN PLACE during those days on the Thessalian coastline across from Euboea. The lone guard of the little Church of the Virgin Mary was captured and tortured with scalding olive oil by three filthy thugs wearing *foustanelles*. He was forced to hand over the meager treasury and the sacred vessels from the altar.

It was possible that the criminals, in fleeing the anticipated pursuit by the Turkish authorities, were able to cross over with a small craft to the Euboean shore. When informed by the Greek ambassador in Volos, the government telegraphed the subprefect and the lieutenant of the police force of Xirohori and told them to take appropriate measures. Almost all of the available policemen were then dispatched to the dangerous regions, and the deputies in the coastal villages were ordered to organize armed villagers into nighttime patrols. But the bandits, luckily for them, had not left the soil of Thessaly, and they were never apprehended, since they were not hunted there.

On one of those days, it was September of 187–, Sergeant Karakitsos, who oversaw five policemen, came and found lodgings in the village. The deputy billeted the policemen, and we accommodated the sergeant in a manor. Tall and broad-chested, he was from Karpenisi. Having served in the military for twenty years, he had acquired the military bearing that characterizes older noncommissioned officers. His head was round and his hair closely cropped, unlike his beard, which was as dense as a forest and long, only shaved a little at the cheeks; a martial and upright mustache and close-knit eyebrows; eyes of a vulture, and a heavy voice like the thump of a drum. A smile seldom stretched his wide lips. But whenever he did smile, all the previous fierceness was effaced from his countenance and an expression of benevolence bathed his features. The relentless guard of public order was suddenly transformed into a venerable abbot.

At other times fleeting and never frequent, this transformation persisted throughout dinnertime. Karakitsos would leave his gun with the bayonet hanging from it in a corner. Removing his hat in order to take a seat before the roasted piglet and a bottle of blond muscatel, he relinquished the symbols of duty and all of their accompanying severity. He was merry company, most talkative, becoming poor company only while the food and drinks were being served—truly like a hungry lion.

It is understandable that the main topic of conversation during dinner was bandits. And the sergeant, over two glasses of wine, mentioned related episodes of his long service, including pursuits of and encounters with gangs of robbers.

"Do you see this scar here?" he asked, showing the top of his head as he was relating a story about a scuffle in Fiotida. "It is from the sword of Karagounis. If a soldier had not managed to grab his arm as he was bringing down his sword on my head from behind a rampart, I would have been done for. But you see, he was written on Charon's list and not I. Half dazed with blood in my eyes, I gave him a pistol shot in the chest and he collapsed to the ground like a bull."

He said this simply, with composure and without bragging, as if it referred to commonplace and insignificant matters. After a while he added: "Of all those monsters, those murderers, my soul took pity on only one.

"When I saw the executioner lay this man in the guillotine, I said to myself: What a pity to sever such a beautiful head!"

"Was he such a handsome man?" I asked.

"An angel! And it was from his beauty that he took his name: they called him Angel John. An angel in appearance and a demon at heart! On top of all the evil things his black soul did, because of his beauty he also had the fate of an unlucky girl from Spolaita on his head. Now, I'll roll a cigarette and tell you how it happened. You will see if it does not resemble the romances that the French write and that are performed in the theaters of Athens."

Eagerly we ignored the silverware on the table and riveted our eyes on Karakitsos. But he was taking his time, rolling the cigarette and taking from his breast pocket a small cigarette holder made of bird bone. He fitted the cigarette carefully into its end.

He proceeded to light it from a smoking lamp; repeatedly drawing and gulping, he puffed clouds of thick smoke from his nostrils. He then rubbed his hat-marked forehead several times with the palm of his hand and, finally meeting our curious gazes, smiled and with lively gestures began the story.

The sixth of November of this year will be thirteen years exactly since that night. I was a countryside policeman in the unit of Trihonia and was on detail with the tax collector. We patrolled the outskirts of the villages. Robbery was epidemic at that time, and the people's lives were unsettled. A few days earlier in Zapanti they had arrested a tobacco merchant. The mobile units had shot at the robbers, killing one, Katsikis. They said that Angel John was also injured, but they were not able to catch him alive. Had the other thieves carried him off on their shoulders, or was he holed up in the forest by Platanorema? Nobody knew. The soldiers were scouring the land, following the trail of blood (for there was a bounty on his head of 2,000 drachmas), but in vain—in vain. On that night—the sixth of November of '65—we came with the tax collector, Mr. Meletis, to Spolaita. It was devilishly cold. The sky was cloudy and a thin sleet was falling. We stayed in the house of Lambros Gikas, the richest man in the village. While waiting for dinner, we dried our wet clothes by a roaring fire. Another landowner of the village, a middle-aged man, Miltos Keramidis, entered. His wife was from Karpenisi and I knew him a little. "Good evening, Mr. Collector," he said. "I see you have made yourself at home here. But I was wondering—since Karakitsos is from the same town as my wife and he's happened to pass through these parts . . . might I take him to my house to talk this evening?" The collector replied, "Karakitsos does not have an assignment until tomorrow morning. He is free to do whatever he wants."

When we reached Miltos's house, he closed the door tightly and whispered in my ear, "Good luck brought you to Spolaita tonight."

"What do you mean?"

"Shhhh! . . . I know Angel John's hideout. He is wounded in the right side and his comrades have abandoned him. In the dead of night, the two of us will go to shoot him like a rabbit in its den. Shhhh! . . . A thousand drachmas in the money belt for each of us."

It appeared as if the heavens had opened before me, and I went to kiss Miltos! One thousand drachmas in the purse of a countryside policeman was something, not to mention the honor and the promotion!

Miltos had no male children, only a daughter, Katerina, seventeen years old, slim and beautiful as cool water. Mrs. Keramidis was away with an in-law who was giving birth. His daughter prepared dinner, but to tell you the truth, that night I did not notice the food or the wine. My mind was on the thousand drachmas and the sergeant's insignia.

While we ate, we talked about the job with half-concealed words, so that the girl would not understand and become worried about her father. But she was looking at us with a peculiar expression as if she understood, and she was so bewildered that her hands were shaking and she dropped an earthenware dish. Miltos did not notice, but I observed it. It is the business of a policeman to see everything! I said to Miltos:

"Why don't you send the girl to bed? What do we need her for?"

"True," he said. "Katerina, take yourself off to bed!"

Katerina bowed her head, said good night, and went into the adjoining room, locking the door behind her.

But how could we pass the time? It seemed like a year. I smoked cigarette after cigarette as I paced up and down. Miltos, much calmer, slept lightly on a mat on the floor with one eye open. After a long while my watch showed that it was ten-thirty.

"It is finally time," I told Miltos.

"Time," he said.

He unhooked his gun from the peg and peered at the flame in the oil lamp. He put a pistol in his leather belt. I took only my carbine; I left my sword behind so it would not clatter and get caught in the branches. In my belt I always kept a small double-barreled pistol that an English lord had given me as a gift. A choice piece.

Wrapped in capes from head to toe, we went slowly out into the darkness. It was raining steadily. Nothing could be heard other than the rain as it dripped on the roof tiles and the paving stones. Miltos went first, and I followed close behind. We took a path that sloped downward, and then we went off at a tangent into the thickets. Miltos paused. I drew near him.

"Here we are," he said quietly in my ear. "He is hiding here behind the boulders in Wolf Cave. We'll approach crouched down next to each other with our guns raised. If he gets wind of us and shoots first, we'll shoot together in the direction of the gun flash. If he seems not to suspect anything, shoot when I shoot."

We proceeded just as he instructed. I raised the hammer of the rifle, pressing the trigger so as not to make any noise. And with my gun aimed, I followed Miltos. He walked on my right with small, short steps. Suddenly he stepped on a dry branch and it snapped. Before I had a chance to tell Miltos that I saw something in the dark start at the noise

. . . *Bam!* I heard next to me. *Bam!* I, too, shot straight ahead.

As soon as he emptied his gun, Miltos struck with the sword. He suspected that if the thief had not been killed instantly he would attack us. Immediately I found myself beside him. I stepped on a body wrapped in a cape, which had collapsed in a heap on the ground. Miltos was beating the body blindly. I kicked it and it rolled like a bag.

"Don't dull your blade in vain," I told him. "It's already a corpse . . ."

It continued to rain. Miltos had brought a torch with him; he took out his flint and lit it. I was waiting expectantly with my foot on the body, the double-barrel pistol in my hand aimed right at it. If it moved, I would plant two bullets into it. But the dead no longer stir, unless they become vampires.

Bending over, the lighted torch in his hand, Miltos approached the body and lifted the cape. Virgin of Prousa! The body we had in front of us was not Angel John. It was . . . it was Katerina, his daughter!

With a moan the poor father fell like a wounded bull upon the lifeless and bloody body. The torch went out on the wet earth.

Suddenly I did not know where I was. I became unhinged. I was petrified there, listening to Miltos's moans. Abruptly, without a word to him, without doing anything at all sensible that could have entered my mind, I took off like a madman. For some time I wandered in the thicket, with no idea where I was going. After a while I began to come to my senses. I thought about going to the village to tell them the news. But instead, unable to find my way, I just made circles and more circles in the dark. After a while I saw the houses whitening the sides of the mountain and the river Aspropotamos shining below. Then I stepped up my pace, finally arriving out of breath. As soon as I reached the village I paused to catch my breath and then let loose two gunshots in the air and began to shout:

"Villagers, help! Help!"

People stirred. Dogs were barking. I made them understand what had happened. Twenty, thirty people grabbed their weapons and ran to Wolf Cave. I did not have the strength to go with them. Miltos's wife heard about the killing of her daughter and fainted dead away.

Talking and shouting, the tax collector and the other villagers gathered around me. Nobody could understand how Miltos's daughter ended up in the spot where Angel John should have been.

It was almost daybreak when the first of the young men who had gone to the cave returned. And he brought three pieces of news: Katerina had been killed by a bullet that had pierced her heart, and she also had five stab wounds; Miltos had lost his power of reasoning; and they had caught Angel John alive, a little ways on from the place where Miltos's daughter had been killed.

In a while the others came. They carried poor Katerina into the house and laid her down. The thief, bound and pale, bowed his head and looked at the lifeless body. The murderer, that beast, had tears in his eyes. When they found him, he offered no resistance. On his own, he had thrown down his weapons from his belt, crossed his hands, and said:

"Now kill me, brothers!"

Since there was no other authority in the village, they turned him over to the mayor and me. I asked him: "Hey you, how was it that they found the girl in your hiding place?"

He answered me clearly: "As my comrades left me wounded, I thought that I would die like a dog in the cave. I spent a day and a night without any food or water. I was expecting Charon to offer me relief, and several times I put the gun in my mouth. But I lost my nerve—would that I hadn't! Suddenly, at the second dawn, I heard footsteps outside the cave. I will cry out, I said to myself, and whatever happens, let it happen! The frightened voice of a girl replied to my feeble utterance. There, where I was waiting for Charon to take my life, I saw Katerina coming to *give* me life. At first she was scared, but after a while she took heart. She brought me food, water, a cloth for my wounds, and ointments. She came every day on her way to see to her flock and tended me. Truly she took pity on me—the poor soul! Tonight as soon as I had closed my eyes, I heard Katerina's signal: two pebbles hit together three times and then again three. I realized that she must be bringing me bad news, at such a late hour and in such weather. "For God's sake," she told me, "you must go away and disappear! My father knows that you are here, and tonight he will come with a policeman to take your head." Leave? How could I leave when I could not even move my leg? She lifted me in her arms and dragged me as far as she could from the place I had lain. She returned to the cave to remove my belongings so that nothing would be found."

As the wounded thief recounted this story with trembling voice, suddenly the door opened and Miltos came inside.

I will never forget the sight of him. His eyes wild, hair every which way; his beard, his hands, his clothes soaked with his daughter's blood.

He was crazy for four months. Eventually he recovered, but he remained a hypochondriac and he died two years later, with Katerina's name on his lips. God delivered me from the weight I might have had on my conscience. My bullet had only hit the sleeve of the cape. Katerina was killed by her father's hand.

Translated by Cynthia Hohlfelder

The Dogs of Seikh-Sou

Yorgos Ioannou

NOW THAT MY DREAM of living in a ground-floor apartment has been realized, only the motorbikes and cars keep me awake at night—the trucks in particular. This, however, is a problem for all those who live in our city, even those living higher up. It isn't a problem that will ever be solved, unless we tear everything down and start building from scratch. But this solution cannot be contemplated, nor should it be.

In the older days we were supposedly disturbed by the roosters crowing, but now we seem to have annihilated them pretty effectively and succeeded merely in depriving ourselves of a rare aesthetic pleasure. What's particularly funny is that in our schools and intellectual circles we persist in accusing the inhabitants of ancient Sybaris of leading the soft life when after all they had not done anything we're not doing ourselves. At any rate, in our own rural Sybaris, on the Peninsula, proud cockerels of all kinds still

Seikh-Sou is a wooded hill used as a public park by the people of Thessaloniki.

exist. I go out there and admire them whenever I get a chance.

At some point, during the occupation, the roosters had returned in all their glory, but our liberation from the Germans brought about their permanent disappearance. Tourism, this new and unbearable occupation that followed, proved fatal for roosters, not to mention what it did to our pride. Oh, well . . .

Since the noise of traffic in those days abated very early in the evening, all loud cries, even the most distant ones, could be heard terribly clearly. As you lay awake you could follow the crowing of the roosters as it spread from one neighborhood to the next. One moment it was the cocks of Varna, next those of Neápolis, Stavroúpolis, Nea Meneméni, Ramóna, then Paleós Stathmós, Koulé Kafé, Kássandros and St. Demétrios, Evangelístra, Saránta Eklissiés, Toúmba and Triandría. It was a comfort of sorts, a kind of communication, something the ferocious military governor could not put a stop to. Once again we'd started to talk about the weather and its variations. It was only in the snotty neighborhoods—Tsimiskí, Paralía, and Metrópolis —that no roosters crowed even in those days. I felt sorry for the people who lived there. An old witch we had at home, when exorcising some evil, would command it three times to "go where no cock crows."

The truth of the matter is that, mingled with the crowing of the roosters, we'd often hear a hoarse voice screaming through a megaphone into the deep night. We hardly ever made out the actual words the plucky kid was striving to get across, but we knew only too well where he would end up, and we all whispered along with him, "Down with

fascism. Freedom for the people. Amen." We'd cross ourselves, feeling somewhat more calm. "God bless your lips,
my boy," I heard my grandmother whisper one night.

Then came the time when, along with the roosters crowing and the megaphones, a clamor of howling and barking
sounded in the night. It wasn't the barking of our neighborhood dogs. There were only a few of those left, and they
were quite weak. Besides, their bark was different. Sweeter
somehow. The new outbursts were numerous and much
more savage, and they were always preceded by a deep
howling chorus that spread over our city, making us freeze.
We set our ears to the window trying to figure out where
it came from. We sat on one another's beds discussing the
new calamity that had befallen us. If it were a raid with
police dogs, God help those poor souls. But the barking
continued insistently, always from the same direction, from
the distant Seikh-Sou, the pine-covered hill. This was a
relief of sorts. But by noon everyone in the neighborhood
knew that the conquerors had set up a training camp for
bloodhounds on the hill. What next! Our terror became
even greater. Those dogs, of course, were meant for us.
They were being trained to hunt us down, to root us out
and tear us to pieces. They were being taught to know our
smell and to follow our tracks. And we sure stank in those
days—something awful. Anyway, the guerrilla war was in
full swing by then and every decent Greek was involved in
the resistance in one way or another.

Our information was soon added to and confirmed. The
dogs would howl at certain times; daybreak was one of
them. That was the time when most raids and arrests took
place—a savage hour. Bundled under our worn covers,

sleepless from worry and hunger, we'd hear them sending over the sprawling city of St. Demétrios a deep, full-throated howl, which ended in many sharp barks.

And to think that only a few years had passed since the time when I'd lie awake in the mildness of the night listening for my father's signal on the whistle of his steam engine, when he was on shunting duty at the station. How I would thrill at the sound of the three or the five short blasts coming from the west and spreading over a city oblivious to their meaning. The whistles were exclusively for me. The three blasts were: *Yo-ri-ka.* And the five blasts: *Yo-ri-ka-ki-mou.* When he whistled five times it meant that I should go to the station in the morning—he usually wanted something.

After war was declared, signaling with train whistles could not even be contemplated. Those who earned a living being suspicious had rolled up their sleeves and taken charge of our destinies. How could one begin to explain to the German military types, or even to the homegrown variety, that three blasts of the whistle mean *Yorika,* and *Yorika* is an affectionate form of *Yorgos,* George, and that five blasts say *Yorikaki mou,* which is even more affectionately *my little Yorgos,* and means go to sleep now and come to me in the morning?

Those dogs had another habit. They howled more when there was a moon. They'd set up a howl to which there was no end—you'd think they were singing. So on several occasions they ruined some beautiful and original musical evenings which we Aryans had started to organize after the rounding up of the Jews in our neighborhood.

Since the curfew started very early in the evening, when

the weather was mild and there was moonlight, we'd sit on the balconies or the flat roofs and hold conversations across the street or connecting yards. We kids would play word games and solve riddles long distance. On the third floor, across the street from our house, lived a girl with a particularly lovely voice. As soon as we caught sight of her in the moonlight, we'd start cajoling for a song. After demurring coyly for the required interval, she'd stand up in her white nightgown, lean on the railings of the old-fashioned balcony, and there, surrounded by grandmothers, mother, sisters, and brothers, she'd start to sing. Immediately all other sound would cease. Our hungry, terrified, orphaned souls would listen with veneration to the lovely voice rising in the summer night. Even the German patrols would stop in the street below, reverently hearing out the song. The girl was a soprano and she sang snatches from operas, Mozart by preference. As soon as she came to the end there would be a roar of applause and cries of "encore." It was then that you'd realize how many had been listening. A few days later we heard applause from as far off as Bit-Pazar, that is to say, the flea market, a different neighborhood altogether. But then we learned to our satisfaction that the entertainment there was being provided by a cabaret *artiste,* and the audience, from what I heard from my friend Angelos, was quite rowdy and made fun of the poor soul—they even rang bells while she was singing. So we were not only the forerunners, we were also the best. But one night, just as Vilma was in the middle of our favorite Greek song and her voice was fluttering through the words

I don't ask for jewels nor do I ask for gold,

the howling started on Seikh-Sou sounding closer than ever, and there was no end to it. At first the girl persisted, but eventually she fell silent and went inside. We all retreated, closing the shutters behind us in an attempt to close out the clamor. A gentle breeze was blowing from the direction of the hill.

A few days later the underground organization of our school appointed me and two other kids to keep track of the activities in Seikh-Sou. We'd keep an eye on the place while pretending to play ball.

I was very familiar with the hill and loved it more than the other two did. The dogs, about two hundred of them, were fenced inside a barbed wire compound on the exact spot where we had always had our lunch before the war, when I went on picnics with my family. Each dog was tied separately—one dog for each pine tree. At the foot of each tree was a doghouse made of planks. The patch of pine needles and the reddish earth where we'd usually spread out our lunch was fouled and inaccessible. A lady of our acquaintance, a Mrs. Evdoxia, lived nearby and every now and then she would invite us over. The dogs were looked after by half a dozen beat-looking and elderly German soldiers. They howled when their mealtime was approaching. As soon as they saw the soldiers carrying the food they would start barking joyously. We'd look in their direction stealthily. Who knew what terrible bites they could inflict with those pointed teeth so busily tearing into the suspect meat? The great brown ants that ran so fast also bit savagely —I still remember them. Ants like that can't be found anymore. The dogs would eat, then piss, and fall clumsily asleep in the shade. On the first day of Lent, we'd deck ourselves out in fancy dress and go to visit there. Panos, the husband of Evdoxia, would make their costumes with the greatest patience, stitching thousands of feathers onto the cloth. He would be a rooster or something like that. Evdoxia was always a hen. And she was always laughing her cackling laugh. She's gone too—it's been several years now. They were a jolly pair; came from Constantinople. One year before the war started the elderly couple had been forced to give up these antics. The sons-in-law were very modern and despised such lower-class customs. It's a well-known fact that dogs, too, hate masqueraders.

We reported all the information about the dogs to our leader, and he was pleased.

Yet we continued our games at Seikh-Sou because, except for the dogs, everything was beautiful there, and my two pals wanted to watch the courting couples, who scurried into the trees before it got too dark. Those were ideal times for Peeping Toms of all kinds. Everything took place in broad daylight and was visible from a distance. Fine young boys would scuttle from tree to tree, from rock to rock, trying to get as close as they could unobserved to the couples who, often stark naked, were indulging in the games of love. There was no vice squad or anything like it in those days, and the laws protecting public decency had been forgotten. Even from the central quay you would see young men swimming stark. Yet as soon as the howling of the dogs started, the sight of the naked couples and the lurking Peeping Toms suddenly became savage. As if everything was being erased.

My friends once persuaded me to accompany them in stalking a young couple. They refused to believe that I wasn't in the least interested. I can still remember the young man striving to convince the reluctant maiden, saying loudly, "Come on now, don't be so old-fashioned." Those two must be at least fifty today, and I do hope they're alive. Whenever I find myself using this argument with a girl it is more as a memorial to that moment in the past than something I actually believe. It is, at any rate, quite effective.

One day the barking suddenly ceased. My father said the dogs had been taken to the mountains—Olympus, Vermio, Cholomon—to hunt down the guerrillas. Poor Germans, they'd no idea what it meant to be up against the Macedonian peasant. . . .

As winter approached we'd hear only the roosters again, and the megaphone and the peacocks from Tsaous-Monastiri, the Byzantine monastery in Thessaloniki, which that dear man the abbot, who was also the gym instructor of the upper town, bred with such tender care.

The peacocks can still be heard at night, when the weather is changing. Those are the only voices that reach us nowadays. Sometimes I absentmindedly get up to go to another bed and chat quietly about the voices with some member of my family. All exquisite things happen only in dreams nowadays. Oh, yes, *The Magic Flute*—that was what Vilma used to sing.

On the dome of the Rotunda of St. George,* pictured in the mosaic, are the most beautiful peacocks one could ever imagine, true birds of paradise. Had those birds lived they

---

*The Rotunda of St. George is a circular Roman building converted into a church by the Byzantines in the fifth century.

would not have squawked like their brothers, since their feet are not ugly. Really, the old people say, and it may even be true, that the peacock lets out that desperate cry when he looks down and sees his common, chicken feet. I don't find the cry of the peacock so ugly. May they squawk eternally while I sleep.

I hadn't been to Seikh-Sou in many years. There had been that nasty business of the killers.* The bastards didn't confine themselves to rape but actually killed the lovers, beating them savagely with rocks. What was worse, they'd attracted to the area swarms of gendarmes and civilian guards, drafted for the occasion, so as soon as you set foot in the woods they'd pop up and ask for your identity card. If you happened to be young they hauled you off to headquarters right away for questioning, and you'd lose the rest of your day and above all your good spirits. It isn't easy to try to explain to people that you'd been suspected of the Seikh-Sou murders and that's why you'd stood them up.

But now that all this had been over—in a manner of speaking—for a long time, I decided to go up there and see the place once again. In vain. Twice recently I wasn't permitted to enter the woods, and for no apparent reason. Somehow I don't think it's very likely that they're training dogs. The first time I had a girl with me, and we wanted to go up to the café. An armed military patrol blocked our path. The soldiers' bright eyes were devouring the girl in the dark. I heard a young man who was stopped as we were leaving say, "*Verboten*, boys, *verboten?*" I doubt that he could

---

*The reference is to a series of brutal murders of lovers in Seikh-Sou, which remained unsolved for years.

have known of those dogs from the past. On the way back I felt awful. It was like having strangers blocking the entrance of your home. The accent of the one in command made things even worse. He sounded like a Peloponnesian, though he might have been from Crete. They're the ones giving orders these days. Only God knows for how much longer.

The second time, it was evening once again, I was going up with a German, one of *us* of course, a fine man, to show him the view of the city. At some turn of the road we were stopped by a group of men wielding flashlights. "Turn back," they shouted roughly. "Entry is forbidden." The German turned the car around and we made our way back. All the way he was blasting away at us and at the world in general for allowing such things to happen. "It's unheard of—*verboten* to enter the woods!" he kept saying over and over again. What could one say? Where could one begin? Could one speak of the original masters of the *verboten*? Could one tell him the story of the dogs, about the Red House (a place outside Thessaloniki used by the Germans for executions), and the rest of the executions? Who among us had the right to be indignant? I chose to say nothing. He's a good lad, one of us, as I said.

Now I only hear the voices inside me. Outside there is nothing any longer. Not even the howling of the dogs. Everything is muffled and dark.

Translated by Calliope Doxiadis

America Is No Longer Here

Yiorgos Chouliaras

WHEN I WAS LITTLE and tourism was not big, foreigners attracted our attention in Greece. That is why I
concluded that I, too, must become a foreigner when I
grew up. I thought I would achieve this by going to America as soon as I had finished high school. My mother raised
no objections, apparently because of the dictatorship—not
because it imposed constraints on freedom of speech,
which it did, but because she must have thought: Better in
Oregon than in jail. Not that the dictatorship was in the
habit of imprisoning graduates of Anatolia College, as my
U.S.-accredited private secondary school was called. Usually students who failed to enter engineering or medical
school joined their father's business, an inevitable development for those who had devoted a considerable part of
their student career to partying or party politics. These
consequences were avoided or at least delayed if graduates
went to America.

Texts read as autobiographical fragments partly confirm the
existence of authors.

"That is where I would go in your place," our very competent Greek teachers implied, even if they did not say it. For without a police-endorsed certificate of nationally correct views, they could get neither a job in a public school nor a passport to travel abroad. Under these immobilizing circumstances, a small group of us older students had secretly assisted a recently hired teacher to draft a compulsory speech for the anniversary of the national revolution, as the military regime liked to call the coup that had brought the colonels to power. In a school auditorium full of suspicious ears, the speech should not appear to dispute the dictatorship, and yet at the same time it should not compromise the speaker's contextually subversive views. This was an instance of Caesar's wife needing to avoid the appearance of an action without avoiding the action itself. Or something like that. Indeed, it was hard for us to recall the proper relation between appearance and reality as formulated in the Latin proverb, a language we were not taught. Our section of the class was defined as practically or scientifically oriented, which meant we dealt with topics such as physics and chemistry in a predominantly theoretical manner, instead of being drilled in languages in an entirely practical manner, which was the case in sections of the class defined as theoretically oriented.

Any good student who left for America during those years escaped from not only the military junta but also the Polytechnic. Contrary to rumors about a lack of correspondence between education and society in Greece, the exact opposite is true. Today, for example, many media-stimulated young people wish to channel themselves accordingly, and college programs in media studies hasten to oblige. At that time, Greek universities, perfectly in tune with the economy, played to the desire of students to engineer a career with a degree from the Polytechnic, whose principal function was to generate civil engineers for the housing boom. (The decade of the sixties was an orgasmic period in home building, though it preceded the climax of the sexual revolution.) The intellectual measurements of Polytechnic alumni were revealed later, however, when, having become superfluous overseers of a collapsing construction sector, many were forced to turn to other skills. A disproportionate number of engineers in Greece became involved in the fine arts or left-wing politics.

Besides my mother's anxiety about people like me getting too involved in anti-junta activities, other family reasons favored my going to America. As everyone knows, any argument that supports a hypothesis can easily be supplemented by additional ones of subsidiary significance. A perhaps divine example involves the comment attributed to an archbishop of Paris—Balzac's contemporary, I presume —that, besides being the Son of God, Jesus also came from a good family on his mother's side. In relation to the facts related here, my father was favorably disposed to my departure with a scholarship for Reed College. He must have assumed that I would return soon, influenced by his own two graduate stints on the North American continent. He did not take into account, however, that he was older than I—when he went, I mean, leaving behind his wife with a successor in her arms. Perhaps he also had in mind the example of our American teachers. Many of these highly mobile scholars came to Greece for only a few years and then returned to their home, or at least left ours.

But why was it that I wanted to go? The presence of teachers from America was a moving experience and advertisement for their country. One might have expected the contrary, at least from students who had acquired sufficient English not only to speak but also to listen. These peripatetic instructors, with the much greater (in comparison to Europeans) honesty that characterizes the average American, used to confide in us that they had come to Greece in order to escape America. But where it was they had wanted to escape from—this excited our imagination further. Even if with touching inaccuracy, we could grasp Europe all the way to England, isolated though it believes itself to be in its island complex. But America—despite the fact that we had heard so much more about it—remained entirely elusive.

Moreover, I thought, if someone were to go to college at the time of the Roman Empire, should not that person have gone to Rome rather than to Athens in order to understand how the world was governed? Correspondingly, shouldn't someone from Greece go to the United States rather than to Great Britain after 1947, the year when the American president known in Greece by his doctrine proclaimed the doctrine known worldwide by his name? Thus I concluded that I should give up the scholarship I had been awarded to go to Oxford. The especially likable director of the British Council in Thessaloniki looked dumbfounded if not annoyed when I declared, surely without revealing my reasons, my intention to go to America. A few years later he passed away—through no fault of mine, I am certain.

I found myself in America barely two weeks after Woodstock, though not quite on account of it. And [t]here* I have remained, again not quite in anticipation of, yet through the twenty-fifth-anniversary celebration of that, after so many years, historical concert. This chronology of events also confirms my presence during the five-hundred-year anniversary of the so-called Discovery—if not of America because of Columbus (for whose television role as a maritime detective I consider Peter Falk ideal), then of Columbus (as well as Colombo) because of America.

On anniversaries of discoveries, it is natural to debate heatedly whether a person can in fact discover a continent on which people had been living for centuries. On the occasion of America's Discovery celebration, the editor of a literary magazine in Athens had thought of publishing a special issue entitled "America Was Always There." I was willing to contribute to the issue, I told our common friend who informed me of the plan, but, due to radical changes since I had discovered America, the title of my contribution could only be "America Is No Longer Here."

Perhaps it was not clear when I left Greece. Later, however, there could be no doubt that Greece is a place where foreigners dream of staying permanently. Accordingly, anyone who is living abroad and considering the possibility of moving to Greece is likely to be a foreigner. This definition, however, is contested by others who do not turn a deaf ear when audibly asked: But did you come to America to become Greek? My case involves a generation of Greeks who experienced at some point the unfulfilled wish to

---

*Whether the author is here or there depends on where the reader is standing.

become foreigners. But America is no longer what we did not know—America is no longer itself—while the rest of the world has become American. Is it conceivable that only by returning to Greece one can relieve oneself of those features of difference that would satisfy a Greek who wanted to be a foreigner but found it impossible to become a foreign Greek? I cannot answer this question with any degree of authority before returning to Greece and beginning to deal with America.

Adapted from the Greek by the author and Artemis Leontis

The Fountain of Brahim-Baba

Elli Alexiou

SINCE THE FOUNTAIN was only two steps from our door, why would we want to pay to have them put running water in the house? Our father used to say: "We make do with the road for a front yard and the water's on the road. So it's the same as if the water was in the house." And mother, who was content with the little she had and never asked for more, used to say: "It'd be insane to have a river running at our feet day and night and us go paying for a skinny pipe that'll run when it pleases. One day they say it's on at two in the morning and the next it's five sun-up . . ."

It was a marble fountain. Over the top rose three humped arches ending with a dome at the back, like the apse of a church, and all kinds of garlands and old inscriptions. From the left and right of the fountain two bright white shelves extended like open wings, and in front was a parapet of marble lacework that gave cover to the traveler when he stopped to drink or wash.

The lettering at the back rose high off the surface, and it, too, looked more like embroidered lace and patterns than writing, because it was Turkish. The craftsman who chiseled it out of the marble had covered the background with a substance that glittered like golden turquoise, and painted the letters red and green. The fountain of Brahim-baba really looked more like a toy. It looked like the needle-work of skilled hands, embellished with love, not like something for everyday use.

For hours at a time it was deserted; it dried up completely and we kids would wonder: "Could they have cut off the water?"—and we'd go over and try to turn it on. At other times it was impossible to get near it. Water carriers and maidservants surrounded it, pushing and shoving, making it all muddy. They set their water jugs on the fountain's shelves and stepped all over the marble lace with their feet. At those times we kids were pushed off to one side and were made to wait. But it really seemed it was made more for us, and once it emptied out and there was room, all we neighborhood kids rushed back to it and ducked in under its lovely arches. I'd stride past the embroidered parapet and go right inside to be closer to the water.

It had a precious spout and faucet made of bronze, also artistically decorated; and though on occasion it might get stolen, it was never long before another one took its place, unless the theft occurred in the evening. Then the fountain flowed like a river throughout the whole night, and the water tumbling on to the plaques could be heard right up to our house. My mother suffered from a heart condition and always had difficulty sleeping and until she fell asleep I'd hear her tossing and turning alongside me, saying to herself: "Though I never tire of your murmuring waters, it breaks my heart to hear you going to waste." In the middle of the night I'd hear her utter these words and they would spread sorrowfully through my breast.

At that time I believed the fountain of Brahim-baba

loved me more than anyone else in the world. One day my
mother pulled out one of my baby teeth with a string and
told me to find a mouse to give it to so that he would
exchange it. I took the tooth and went out into the street.
It was exactly midday, well into the summer, and the street
was deserted. I went to the fountain, strode past the parapet, and sitting on my haunches inside, threw my tooth
into the hole where all the water ran out. Then I hummed
the song my mother taught me earlier:

> *Mousey, take this little tooth*
> *And give back one of iron,*
> *So I can clomp stale bread and crusts*
> *And nibble on hard rusks.*

I had once seen a frightened mouse run circles inside the
fountain, and finally he shot off and dashed into the hole,
and from then on I believed that that was where he had his
nest.

One day when on my way home, I saw people gathered
in front of the fountain. It was a mixed group, Turks with
their red fezzes, and Greek Christians, and they were looking at the golden inscriptions which till then I had taken
for pretty designs.

One old Turk, a venerable figure with spectacles, stood
in the middle. He looked at the inscription, read the Turkish out loud, and then explained it in Greek. And everyone
listened with fixed attention and seemed very sad; I
stopped and listened:

"These are lines from the Koran: *'la ilaha il Allah wa
Muhammada rasul Allah*. There is only one unique God

and Muhammad is His apostle' . . . Ah but no, it's not all
from the Koran; there's something else: *yalnız o bilir ve
bahtsız olanları teselli edebilir* . . . He and He alone knows
how to console those in despair, for He has put out the fire
that burned within me and rescued my little Ahmet from
the claws of Death . . . I, Ibrahim, the son of Ahmet, the
obedient servant of God, build this fountain on the road
that the thirsty may quench their thirst and praise the name
of the great Rabbi.'"

Why were the people sad? What the Turk read wasn't
sad. But the evil which befell Brahim-baba was so great the
whole community talked about it and wept. Young and old,
we all learned of it.

Brahim-baba had had this fountain built years ago for his
son. When the boy was three years old he fell ill with a
severe sore throat, and the doctors gave him up for lost. But
Brahim-baba, through the light of God, made a vow to the
Rabbi that he would establish a fountain on the road if only
his son survived. And the boy did live and this lace-
encrusted fountain was built. But yesterday his son was hit
by a car and killed. He had grown up now and was a handsome young man ready for marriage.

Not much time went by after that, when the order was
issued for all the Turks in our area to move to Turkey and
the Greeks from there to move here. At first no one could
believe it. Such a thing was unimaginable. The newspapers
wrote all about it, over and over again, in large striking
headlines, and the Turks and the Greeks read it together,
gathered here and there, on the street corners and in coffeehouses. But the newspapers just write whatever they
want . . . ! Things like that can't happen. Can you just lift

up a whole people, push them out of their homes, uproot them from their own land? Are they a kind of bundle you just pick up and dump somewhere else? You can draw off oil when it's mixed with water, they said; but you can't separate milk from water. Because after so many years of living with one another they'd grown together through all kinds of bonds, businesses, buying and selling, friendships. They were like two different plants that you raise in the same flower box, and for all that each feels foreign to the other, under the soil their roots have become intertwined, and likewise their branches above ground. If you pull on one to uproot it the other follows after it. Why, people often whispered in your ear that such and such a Turkish girl was in love with a certain Greek, and at Greek funerals without exception you'd see some Turks, bent over in tears, following in the rear with their scarlet fezzes. And if you watched from a high window, the crowd below looked like a plowed field in springtime with red poppies blossoming around the edges.

However, many Turks, the ones with big families, had already begun to move. They sold their things as best they could just to get going, it was said, one hour earlier. Perhaps they could settle in better if they were the first to arrive. In the villages they sold their animals and their oil, because the law was they could only sell their movable property, and, pushing and shoving, they made their way down to the harbor. Our town, which had always been so quiet, was turned upside down. Overnight it was transformed into an auction fair. Old watches under a glass bell, pans that had hung on the same nail for fifty years, were now in the hands of public criers who sought a buyer. And

Zeineb-hanoum had just negotiated her daughter's marriage and sold whatever she had to set her up with her own household. The good mother cashed in her gold Mahmouds and sold her diamond *elmasi*. She'd spent everything to get that little house built. But now she'd be leaving it all as it was, half finished, and they'd depart with no more than their own two souls. They were painting the front windows when the general order arrived, and they left them the way they were, right in the middle. Whoever's fate it is to come and live in the house, let them paint the windows the color they want. For our part, Zeineb-hanoum said, fate would have us wring out our last drop of blood arranging a nook to crawl into, and then at the final hour we're left with nothing but debts.

The Greeks, especially the women, accompanied the Turkish families down to the ship. They held them by the arm or took up the children in their embrace—they tried to find something to do for one another, to do something, and they gave gifts to keep one another in memory. The final round of the ship's whistle was accompanied by a sorrowful murmur and muffled sobs and sighing. And still they went on making requests of one another:

"Be sure to write, Dirayet-hanoum. No excuses—as soon as your Ihsani, God willing, has given birth, and tell me whether it's a boy or a girl. How can you leave like this? We're so worried about you."

"Be happy! When Stavros gets back from the army, write me what he says . . . He'll write me himself, but he may not want to hurt my feelings and tell me the truth. But I don't want to go on with the hope that he'll be able to bring me back if it's just lies."

And they went from one place to the other the whole day through arranging recommendations if they'd been employees, in case, they said, it would do them some good where they were going, and they wanted an official record for their children showing they'd finished the second grade of Greek high school or the fourth grade of elementary school.

Brahim-baba didn't look as if he intended to leave. He neither sold off anything nor did he seem in a rush. Whenever the Turkish ships arrived and loaded up with people, he went down to the harbor as well, along with the Greeks, and followed it all as a spectator. As if none of this affected him personally.

However, this matter had a time limit, and the deadline was in a day or so. Around then, Brahim-baba got up and went to the bishop. This is where he put all his hopes and he felt safe. After all, it doesn't really make a big difference, he must have said to himself; I'll become a Christian.

"Effendi," he said to the bishop, "I can't leave, I don't want to leave. It's that I become a Christian!"

"I understand," the bishop said, "but it's forbidden for us to Christianize those marked for the exchange. What can I do in your case? Another fellow came to me for the same reason."

"I don't speak Turkish. I'm an old man on my own, my *hanoum*'s no help anymore. She just sits at the end of the couch like a ball of yarn. Where should I go? Effendi, for your own part have you ever seen them take someone and root out his heart and then just tell him to get up and walk away? That's the way they want to treat me."

On the last day Brahim-baba didn't have the strength to

restrain himself any longer; he'd done well to hold out so long, but now he gave his heart free rein. He went into the street and wept out loud like a babe—he'd had as much as he could take. He went from one shop to the next in tears and one by one pressed each Greek for an answer:

"Do you have any complaint about me, brother? Have I done you any harm?"

"What harm would you have done me, *bey*? You were a saint throughout the region . . ."

And on the line he would go and ask again: "Boss, have I somehow done you damage without knowing it? Without meaning to?"

What could they reply . . . ?

"If we don't have any quarrel between us and I accept you and you accept me, why can't you write a paper and send it and at least let me stay here? I'm an old man. There's no place for me to go. We can't dig up our people; our religion doesn't allow us, as yours does, to remove the remains of someone recently dead."

A few days later we accompanied them, as well, down to the harbor.

It was a night without moon and a gentle breeze was blowing. The sea was a bit rough; even in the harbor there were waves. At home we felt sorry that along with everything else, the sea would upset the old folks, this poor care-ridden couple. Hariye-hanoum, the old lady of Brahim-baba, walked arm-in-arm with my mother, and my father was behind with Brahim himself. We had told Mother not to come, to stay at home because she would get upset and her heart would give her trouble, but she wanted to come nonetheless.

"I know, my dear," said Hariye-hanoum, "that you can't walk a great distance. But if it should happen that the children pass by the *mazarlik*—the Turkish graves—let them keep their eye on the tombstone of my late son Ahmet. I hand him over to your care. And if it's no great trouble for you, write me; I planted hyacinths and in a few days they'll be in blossom . . . !"

"I'll even go myself. And I'll send the children regularly to water them . . ."

The other Turks didn't care for their people after death; if they were wealthy, they put up an expensive tombstone and that was all. But Hariye-hanoum, like the Greeks, brought her son flowers in a golden vase, lit a candle regularly, and dug up the soil all round and planted it for him.

When we had returned home, my mother stretched out in the armchair. She had trouble breathing. We brought her ether, as always, and put some drops of it in sugar and gave it to her to take. We tried to console her, but we were crying ourselves.

The same week, she sent us to the graveyard to do the watering. We knew the tombstone of Ahmet from other times and picked it out immediately in the midst of that sea, in the midst of the unending expanse of Turkish graves.

We did the watering. We had a bouquet of roses with us. We took out of their vase his mother's now-withered flowers and replaced them with fresh ones. We burned Turkish incense and then left. That same day, as we were leaving, we saw some people in the middle of the Turkish cemetery. They were holding measuring rods and were busy measuring the land, bending down in the midst of the gravestones.

"What are you measuring?"

"The layout for the settlement. There's going to be an urban settlement here."

Within the same year life was kindled in the new settlement, on top of the Turkish bones. All the foundations of the houses were laid on top of skulls and various kinds of human remains. In the streets of the housing settlement, on the freshly dug red earth that had been watered and kneaded with the tears and sorrows of so many generations, the refugee children, unsuspecting, drew squares with chalk and played hopscotch.

Hariye-hanoum went on writing to my mother and would ask the news and my mother wrote back:

"Yes, oh yes; they blossomed this year too."

Translated by Theodore Sampson

Autobiography of a Book

Michel Faïs

*Photocopy No. . . . : Transcribed (imaginary)
interview of Yiannis Ahtalis by Edmond
Bahar.*

YOU TOLD ME over the phone, Mr. Bahar, that you are
working on a book about Komotini. Could you explain to
me, now that we are talking face to face, exactly what it is
about?

—I am collecting material, I am interested in anything:
oral testimonies, diaries, letters, historical or folklore essays,

Editor's note: Balkan Greece forms the background, the poly-
ethnic town of Komotini the focal point of the novel,
Autobiography of a Book. At its narrative center, a young man is
trying to gather enough information to tell the story of his
birthplace—and so somehow to purify himself of a bloody history that includes the "cleansing" of his own family members
on March 3, 1943. The excerpt that follows records an (imaginary) interview with one Yiannis Ahtalis, a native well-versed
in the complex history of relations among Jews, Pomaks, Turks,
Christian and Muslim Greeks, Armenians, Sarakatsans,
Bulgarians, and Gypsies in northeastern Greece.

even photographs or memorabilia concerning Komotini—roughly anything since the Asia Minor catastrophe. Certainly I am not a historian, and consequently I do not have the ambition to write a specialized study. Perhaps in the future this material will take the form of a picturebook.

Interesting, although I am not sure yet in what way I could prove useful to you.

—Simply by talking to me. It is my understanding that you know the history of the city like no one else.

The usual exaggerations. Of course, your statement flatters me and, to be honest, it excites me. It is just that I am afraid I will disappoint you. There are, you know, two or three individuals who could speak better to you, more systematically, than I. Do you know Mr. Ayisilaos Kouloglou? He has the most complete archive of the city. Also Mr. Papazekos, the photographer. His photographs of the old city are wonderful. You can contact them and tell them I sent you. There are also some others, of course, whose names escape me at the moment.

—I have already spoken to both of them.

Did Ayisilaos show you his archive?

—Which archive?

I was going to say, Ayisilaos, Ayisilaos Kouloglou that is, has an obsession with history. Not only with Komotini's history but with Thrace's as a whole. When he was younger, he ventured as far as Vienna. He traveled; he went to "make a bid" in the auction of a 1380 copy of a Byzantine code, which contained some decree about what was then called Koumoutsina. Imagine his passion.

—Mr. Kouloglou told me interesting things while narrating what was basically the history of his family.

Good enough. Generally he is secretive. Did you know the disabled owner of the kiosk by the railway station? Antonis Tarnaras is his name. That was his name, rather, since he is deceased now.

—Very well, since I grew up in the same neighborhood.

Even better. Well, for years he assisted Ayisilaos in the cataloging of his archive. Before that, there were also rumors that Ayisilaos literally saved him from public humiliation and imprisonment. Because of some odd court case.

But let's set this aside. What exactly do you want to ask me?

—I would like to start our conversation with an outline of all the backstage diplomacy that preceded the liberation of Thrace, and particularly of Komotini.

All right. Before we start, however, I would like to clarify something: liberation and incorporation are two different things. And I will explain to you what I mean right now.

In this region, in 1919, intense diplomatic jockeying took place. The Allies, to be sure, requested the holding of some kind of referendum.

The battle was fierce. Finally, Vamvakas prevailed. He was an ingenious diplomat, a close aide of Venizelos. With his connections he managed to win the support of certain influential members of the Jewish community and of the Armenians. Thus, the Armenians openly supported the Greeks, while the Jews remained neutral. Vamvakas also won the support of two representatives of the Turkish side.

Now, why did I differentiate: incorporation—liberation? At the end of the war, in 1919, these areas were occupied by the Bulgarians. They had been ceded according to the treaty of Bucharest.

Upon entering this area, the coalition forces occupied it for the Allies. This automatically liberated us from the Bulgarian yoke. When the final concession to Greece took place, that was incorporation. Incorporation here should not be understood in its narrow sense: unlike the cases of the Dodecanese and the Ionian islands, incorporation in our case involved actual union with the main body of Greece. And rightfully, the proper date for the celebration of this event is May 14.

Because something odd happens here. We hold three celebrations for the liberation: one in Xanthi, on the occasion of the entrance of a British battalion into the city in October 1919; one in Komotini, with the entrance of the French troops in May 1920; and one in Didimotiho, with the entrance of Italian forces in August 1920.

—Is that the reason why there are Catholics in the county of Evros even today?

Levantine Westerners who naturally trace their roots from that point.

—You mentioned the position of the minorities in what you characterized as "some kind of referendum." I would be interested in your particular comments regarding the position of the Armenians and the Jews during that period.

Yes, let's begin with the Armenians. There was a Roupen, a merchant-tailor. He was an important member of the Armenian community who sided openly with the Greek point of view and voted for the election of a civilian Greek governor.

The Jews, on the other hand, since they were mostly involved in trade, could adapt to any environment. Here we

have a bourgeoisie, not manual laborers. As you understand, they could live equally well with either the Bulgarians, or the Turks, or with the French.

Note that in October of 1919 the French officers were
hosted in Jewish households when the Eleventh Greek
Division, along with the advancing French troops—led by
General Sarpy—entered the city. Sarpy and his staff that is.
This was arranged for reasons of security and comfort,
since the Jews were fluent in French. So they were installed
in the mansions of the president and the secretary of the
Jewish community: they were called Nefousi and Romano,
if I recall their names correctly.

Vamvakas therefore deemed that the Jewish support
should be enlisted at any cost. This is why he convinced the
powerful tobacco merchant Karaso—the Jewish representative in the negotiations—to remain neutral.

—I have been told, and I would like you to confirm it,
that around the fortress, in the synagogue near "Olimbo,"
there was a gate that was locked at night and opened in the
morning. That the Jewish district there functioned practically like a ghetto.

This is true. But let's examine the events in order. Before
the war there were no more than three hundred Jewish
families in Komotini. We speak about extended families—
brothers, cousins, brothers-in-law; large families, because
at that time they would marry strictly among themselves.
Assimilation was a taboo.

As they were multilingual, well dressed, and cultured,
they provided a European ambiance to oriental Komotini.

All of what is currently Ermou Street and the Covered
Market was crammed with Jewish stores. You would

mostly see drapery and haberdashery shops. The kind of things that interest women: thread, knitting wool, buttons, underwear—something like a contemporary boutique.

The Turks had almost no involvement with trade. The Greeks and the Armenians were involved, but to a lesser degree.

The community, of course, had the foresight to establish a special fund; they called it Avrathim, and it was designed to assist poor Jews—they would be given meal tickets, clothes, and other supplies.

Now, many children from Greek families attended the Jewish school, since it was the only school in the area where a foreign language—French—was taught. I myself graduated from a Jewish elementary school.

There also existed a Spanish consulate—because the Jews in Thrace, and in northern Greece in general, originated from Spain.

There exists a street that was a Jewish residential area. It is the famous Makkavaion Street, currently named Karaoli —it was an entire district. Inside the fortress there was also the synagogue with scattered Jewish households around it, belonging, however, to families of lower social standing— the Jewish folk, as we called them.

Well, the gate of this Byzantine fortress closed at night and opened at dawn. It was run like a ghetto, as you have correctly heard. In earlier times, as my grandmother used to tell me, certain legends had been created: allegedly inexplicable things happened inside that prevented Christians from entering.

The Bulgarians pulled the gate down later, connecting in this way the street that passes in front of the Old Cathedral with Oikonomou Street—what is the name of the street where the demolished mosque is located?

This was the opening up of the streets during the occupation, in case you have heard the old-timers mention it.

—What do you remember about the day of the Jewish "cleansing," which, if I am not mistaken, took place on March 3, 1943?

Exactly, March 3, 1943. The day of the Bulgarian national celebration, the anniversary of their liberation from the Turks. It was two or three hours before dawn. The temperature was below freezing and it was snowing lightly.

I remember everything precisely as it happened. The Bulgarians took the Jews by surprise. This is because the previous day they had issued a decree ordering the Jews to gather outside the synagogue in the morning, say at seven o'clock. What did the Bulgarians do? Two hours before dawn they lit all the city lights. Shortly after, the streets were filled with cries, shouts, curses. We remained inside our houses, conforming to the imposed curfew, not knowing how to react.

The Bulgarians, of course, had violated the initial agreement, but your people—we should say this—accepted the whole event in complete passivity.

This way the Bulgarians, almost invading the Jewish homes, forced the Jews to dress in a hurry and to pick up only what they could carry in their arms. Afterward, they led them to the synagogue. There, once they counted them, they led them to the railway station, guarding them on both sides. In the clearing of the poplar trees they divided them into two groups.

In charge of the whole operation was Kristo Datsaling,

the commander of the "Bastille," as we used to call the building housing the Security Police; he was the terror of all the inhabitants of Komotini.

Some—the fewest of them, anyway—were transported through Bulgaria to the Danube in large trucks. There, as we found out later, they met a sad death by drowning. The majority, however, were packed like animals into freight cars and shipped to Thessaloniki. From there, according to a story told to me by a survivor named Victor Talvi—he had a small hosiery store on Ermou Street, the back part of which he used as a black-market lira exchange—they forwarded them via express railway to Treblinka and Bürgenau for the "final solution."

The very same individual—today he lives in Haifa—told me an incredible story: that their adopted daughter—was her name Estelle?—collaborated with the Nazis. And that it was essentially she who drove his wife and daughter to the gas chamber by informing against them for an insignificant offense.

And all this happened to Victor, who used to tell me, "A real merchant should pay attention even to the amount of dust on a customer's shoes."

The next day, in order to intimidate the Jews who had been rounded up and to avoid riots, the Bulgarians threatened to execute the wife and young daughter of Louria, the cloth merchant. Imagine, moreover: at the moment they stood them against the wall for the mock execution, the girl bent down twice to dust off her shoes.

This event was told to me by Moschopoulos, who back then was the railway stationmaster, and who after a few months died at the hands of the Bulgarians.

—Were there any survivors?

From a total of about one thousand Jewish inhabitants, it is questionable if there were more than fifteen to twenty survivors.

One of them was the physician Danon. Being a leftist, he took refuge with his family in the mountains—he joined the resistance. Also, the youngest son of the insurance agent Kalvos was among the survivors. He was engaged to the daughter of the Spanish consul, and they passed him off as a Spanish citizen and consulate employee.

The twin daughters of the community's president, Nefousi, also must have escaped the gas chambers. They later settled in Israel.

Finally, there is an unconfirmed account regarding the eldest son of Rabbi Faïs. Nobody knows for certain whether this young man survived in the end. In any case, during the occupation, Pouliasis—the owner of the two big supermarkets—was hiding him in his washhouse.

Anyhow, the day following the expulsion, the market was flooded with liras, rings, necklaces. They were the plunder of the Bulgarian soldiers, who were selling them for anything they asked. In those years the brokers made a fortune.

In the neighborhood where I was born—near Tsanaklio—they were saying that when they started repairing the tile roof of the house formerly owned by the pharmacist Kazi, the project was brought to a halt. And that two years later the master workman became the owner of a three-story building in Xanthi. This was possible because he found a brazier full of medallions and liras that had been stashed in the roof.

Of course, this might also be irresponsible rumor-mongering.

—Perhaps it would be interesting to shift our discussion to the Armenian minority.

With pleasure. Before we proceed, however, I would like to ask you something, too.

—Whatever you like.

You are of Jewish descent, but is it correct that your father is not a native of Komotini?

—That's right, he comes from Drama.

Does this mean that you are not related to the Bahar family in Komotini?

—Perhaps there is a distant connection. You know how complex Jewish lineages can be.

You know, I was a classmate of Bahar's son. Boy, what have you reminded me of now? Sometimes memory spills from everywhere. One plans to say something and ends up saying something totally different. I will not digress again, I promise you. Allow me to indulge only in this tangent.

—As far as I'm concerned, it's the so-called "off-the-subject" topics that are the most interesting. Well, continue . . .

Samikos's father was killed in a car accident. Poor Mr. Leon was the first victim of this kind in our city. It is a paradox that he was hit by another Jew: it was Karaso's son, who was driving the latest Ford model bought from a motor show in Paris. Needless to say, that was an event talked about for months in our city. Naturally this was before the war. Well, Samikos, an uncompromising young man—he played defensive back for Orfea—spent all night at his father's wake along with his kin. The established custom. When he woke up in the morning, what did they see: his hair turned white, like a cocoon. He was only twenty years old; it was because of the distress. You had asked me something, though?

—Yes, you had started telling me about the Armenians.

Yes, there were about five hundred Armenians in Komotini. Let's say six hundred. We are talking after 1922. With time, however, their numbers decreased. There was a strong wave of emigration to the United States. After 1922, those Armenians coming from the depths of Asia arrived in our area in pretty bad shape. Dressed in rags, with nothing.

Habik Mateosian, the watchmaker—he is deceased now, God rest his soul—used to tell me that his mother grabbed him from the cradle just as he was. They came from Prousa. The soldiers provided her with their handkerchiefs so that she could swaddle him on the road. Such was their haste when these people fled.

On the contrary, the Armenians who came from eastern Thrace arrived well organized. They brought money, everything. They even brought their chairs and quilts.

—Where exactly was the Armenian district located?

Behind what is presently the park. You know where City Hall is today? There.

Earlier there were, in a way, two sects. Two fighting parties. They were divided by deep animosity. They would even take their cases to the courts. They wouldn't intermarry. They were the Tashnak, the nationalists, and the Hnchak, the more open-minded as we would characterize them today. The former say that after the 1918 slaughter of the Armenians, the best young men from all the communities would gather in a secret place to cast lots. Whichever Tashnak drew the lot was assigned a sacred mission: to kill a Turkish official.

The Hnchak were from Lebanon, while the Tashnak were from Yerevan, which they recognized as their "mother-seat," as they used to say.

~

—I have heard that we have a high rate of consumption of psychotherapeutic drugs among minority populations; is this the case?

Unfortunately yes. Especially among women, since they have been subjected—in the earlier years to a larger degree —to double oppression from men: social and physical. The Muslim religion is patriarchal to an extreme, as you know. Incidentally, do you know what the Muslim women did when the Bulgarians entered the city?

—No, what did they do?

In a state of fear and despair, they were clattering tin and copper utensils. The whole of Komotini was shaking from the appeals, the anguished cries, and the metallic sounds. It was something grotesque.

—Now that I hear this, someone spoke to me about it, but I do not remember who.

A week after German troops seized the heroic forts of Ehinou and Nimfaias with continuous air strikes and flamethrowers, the Bulgarians started controlling the government services and distributing land to propertyless Bulgarians—with the following hypocritical claim: that since the Greek authorities had abandoned their position, western Thrace could not remain without a leader.

At the same time, they started looting the town of Komotini. And again with the "lawful" pretext that they were searching for weapons, sugar, coffee, flour, beans. Although the Greeks accepted this situation ungrudgingly, the Muslims sought refuge in the surrounding forests. They left the women behind by themselves, with orders not to open the doors to anybody. Because, in fact, there is a rule in Muslim custom prohibiting women to show themselves before strangers.

Respect of rule and custom? What kind of respect are we talking about? The Bulgarians broke into the houses, took their time plundering, and, naturally, raped the poor Muslim women. When the Turkish general consul intervened, it was too late.

~

—When we define minority populations, we must view as another category the Tourkokatsiveli, Gypsies, who inhabit the Teneke neighborhood known as "Pos Pos."

Until 1937, the Gypsies were living in the area where the Department of Health is presently located, across from the Social Medical Welfare Service. You can imagine how they lived. Kalatzis, the general governor of Thrace at the time, decided to relocate them to Pos Pos, which he renamed to the more refined Kalaitzia.

Pos Pos is a variation of the name Vos Vos. It is a Byzantine name. The repetition is perhaps related to Bosporus.

Moreover, note that prior to the Metaxas dictatorship this was an area planted all over with plane trees and featuring three beautiful watermills; it was a place used by the lower socioeconomic classes for excursions and recreation.

Something else that is interesting: some old people had told me that in the first decades of the century they encountered Romiokatsiveli families. These were Gypsies who, although they atavistically practiced their traditional occupations, retained the Orthodox faith they had held since the Byzantine period; they only spoke their Gypsy language while working.

—When I was a child, around 1965, I remember camel

drivers crossing the city. Even now I am puzzled: where did these camels come from, and where were they going?

The camel drivers were Muslims. They had special stables where the government headquarters are presently located. There were no Greeks involved in this business. They mostly transported wood and coal from the mountainous part of Rhodope county, from Pomak villages. Neither donkeys nor mules could easily make it. But the camel could manage.

Now, just how camels were able to carry it off is a bit curious. But perhaps there was a coordinated effort. That is, they would bring the load down by mule to a certain point, and subsequently load it onto a camel.

However, the Sarakatsani caravans offered a similar, and even more phantasmagoric spectacle.

—So that's why the children clapped in the Poalla Theater when the film *Lawrence of Arabia* was shown. It is because they recognized our camel drivers.

—You mentioned two issues that interest me greatly: the Pomak villages and the Sarakatsani.

What can I say about the Pomaks? Everything about them is in flux and they have become a target of contesting national claims by our neighbors. Because here—unfortunately—something much worse has happened: harsh partisan exploitation.

Let us not say more, however, because we will be accused of national treason. Because we Greeks possess this "quality" in excess: first we fight among us and harm ourselves, then we search for scapegoats elsewhere, the so-called "foreign decision centers."

Paparrigopoulos put it wonderfully. I quote him: "Inasmuch as we believe that it is always the other who is at fault, while we alone are infallible, it is difficult to stop sinning."

What should I tell you about the Pomaks? That, according to the Bulgarians, the word *Pomakos* has its origins in the verb *pomangam,* which means to assist; consequently, Pomakos means "one who helps," therefore an ally? What can I tell you? That the Turks consider them remnants of the Petsenegoni and Komani who attacked Byzantium in the fourth century? Or that according to Greek and international historians, they are the most ancient remnant population of western Thrace, inhabiting a large area—from Stavroupoli, including all the mountainous regions, up to Evros county, Megalo Deri. And we see them even today —suspicious, reticent, and insecure—when they come down to the cities to shop.

Honestly, once again I feel the need to refer you to a bibliography. About the Pomaks in particular, I have a vast library from which I can lend you whatever you want.

You know something, though, and you shouldn't take this as an evasion. As far as I am concerned, now that I am at the end of my life, everything that I read about Komotini and all I sought to learn from older people no longer exists. It has vanished. The Komotini I came to know through all these years has been reduced to insignificant little things.

—What kind of little things?

What kind? Let's call them the peculiarities of an old man.

—I don't follow you, Mr. Ahtalis.

Listen. You asked me about the Pomaks, do you know what has been left to me concerning them? A prewar postcard.

A postcard showing the famous Vienna Opera illuminated. Now, what is the connection?

I had an uncle, Filippo—from my mother's side—whom I loved dearly. He was, not to tire you with details, the county's medical physician, and he was visiting the most remote areas of the county. In 1938 he sent us this postcard, signed "Loving Kisses, 606." Do you know why? How could you know; you are so young. It was because of the numerous injections of the drug neosalvarsani—widely known as 606—he administered in those years to syphilitic individuals. And since syphilis decimated the Pomak villages before the war, it was almost as if it were hereditary. Do you follow now?

—Very well. Concerning the Sarakatsani now, what kind of "little things" have you retained?

You tempt me, Mr. Bahar. But let it be; concerning the Sarakatsani I have been left with a taste.

—A taste?

Precisely, a taste. My father had a Sarakatsan friend who would bring us *kousmari* when these people migrated down to their winter quarters. *Kousmari* was an ambrosia, godly stuff. What was it? Soured cheese, milk, flower, and butter —a blend. Shepherd's food. We'd hold a feast in the house. We'd eat it slowly because it made you queasy, with *raki* made from berries.

Unfortunately, a guerrilla group of mixed political persuasion killed this great individual outside of town. Most likely in order to rob him. Tempers back then—it was summer of 1949—were particularly fierce, even though during the leftist control of the area we had a good governor, a moderate individual, named Apostolidis.

—I think that the interview is over, Mr. Ahtalis.

Now, could I ask you something too?

—Please.

Do you plan to make any changes at all in our conversation, in case, of course, you will include it in your book?

—Honestly, I cannot answer you. Particularly at this moment. For instance, the taped monologue of the late Papazekos, except for some linguistic editing, I plan to publish exactly as it is. In other cases, there are so many edits and cross-cuts that the original talk disappears completely. Everything is judged on a case-by-case basis.

All right. I do not suppose that you will publish something that I have told you and expose me. I would like to be fully informed about the excerpts you will select for publication.

—This is understood, Mr. Ahtalis. Still, I wonder. How come you never thought of publishing a contemporary history of Komotini? It would be a pity to waste such voluminous information, such priceless empirical material. So nicely formulated, too, judging from your narration.

Perhaps I was waiting for—you. Look, when I was working in the library, it would have been imprudent, risky, I dare say, to attempt something of that sort. I told you and I showed you what happened with the little volume *Stella Ahtalis: The End of a Myth*. And there I was only writing about a relative of mine. If I were to speak about everybody and everything—

Supposedly when you work for the state—and even more importantly, in a position having to do with education— you ought to refrain from criticism—from the criticism of history and of the everyday. Small-town societies neither forgive easily nor forget quickly.

There is something else, though. Something deeper and, in the final analysis, inevitable. When you narrate the event, the historical event, that is, it becomes a kind of personal experience—even though you have not lived the event in question. Because language mediates. As a result, whoever claims that a particular fact "speaks for itself" is either a liar or naive. And I have been neither. At least, that's what I would like to believe. Let alone the fact that all along I've had a literally pathological obsession with historical accuracy. I considered facts as something sacred.

Besides all this, though, perhaps now that I've retired I'll put some order in my archive. For a book? Perhaps it is too late now. On the other hand, it is perhaps too early suddenly to make that many enemies. Don't you think I still have another ten years to go?

Translated by Yiorgios Anagnostu

The Regards

Alexandra Papadopoulou

THEY BROUGHT US A MAID from Mytilini. She was a Plomaritissa, from Kameno Horio.

When from her window she saw boats passing, she would often leave off her chores, run to the window that faces the sea, and wave her handkerchief; at times she cried, at others she laughed. Then my aunt would reproach her, and she, in turn, would sing couplets of complaint.

I was her secretary. I wrote her letters and read her those that arrived—a few couplets drenched in bitter longing, and then the regards, two pages of them with first and last names of everyone, male and female.

This often seemed to me an unbearable torment, and I would write only half of the names. I did not know then that this was a deceit, that such an omission could have grave consequences. The time did come, however, for me to understand my fault and bitterly regret it.

My uncle, a shipowner renowned in all the beautiful ports of Mytilini, received me for the summer so that I, too, could admire the Moskonisia where olive trees reflect upon the sea, Kidonies with its lively Hellenism, and the magical shores of Mytilini, with its hardworking people.

Amersouda (that was the maid's name) asked me to write a letter for her. But, bless her, she listed so many names and I was in such a hurry that this time I did not write down any of the regards, and only when I saw her kissing the letter and saying, "Tell my *manoula* that I kissed it right here, here right on top of the regards," did I regret it a bit. Still, I hid the letter while she was saying to me, "Konstantella, go to the plane tree of Merena on Sunday to see how the girls swing on the swings and how they sing, and also go to Ayiasotissa the Holy Mother to see real beauty."

I made this, my first journey, in wonderful weather and I encountered magical shores, but I will not describe my trip, only how I went up to Kameno Horio on donkeyback, with my uncle's permission, after I arrived at Plomari. The olive and pine trees were exchanging sweet embraces and shading the well-kept road that unites the river with Kameno Horio. Marble fountains on the road bore the inscription—it's not at my fingertips now, something like: refresh yourself, stranger, and pray for the soul of the one who built this water fountain.

The donkey driver knew Amersouda's family.

"Good people and good householders. The girl left so that they could repay their debt and finish building her home, for in our parts every girl must have a home with a complete household, even woolen covers for the calves; without these, she cannot marry."

We reached Amersouda's home. Her mother, still beautiful, received us on the terrace with affection and emotion. We were offered fruit and *raki*, the local liquor. Then she began with questions about Amersouda.

"Has she grown? Does she remember us? We really love her."

She showed the letter and everyone gathered around the loom, where all the relatives were weaving a multicolored tapestry. The grandmother came, too, with her cane.

Then Margela, a relative, read the letter with its couplets. The old woman sat listening, eating the girl alive with her blurry eyes. But when she did not hear her name mentioned in the regards, she hid her face inside her black kerchief and started to cry bitterly. The godmother, too, an enormous woman—she also grew bitter, but she did not hide it, only said, "Heh, when they leave home they forget everything, village, relative, and friend." Two fat tears wetted her broad face. Around me I saw bitter faces. Around me fluttered a silent curse on foreign lands.

The old lady started to sing her complaint, as it was the custom in this birthplace of Sappho and Alcaeus to sing one's joy and sorrow.

I was conscience-stricken. How was I to imagine that those two pages of regards that I had disregarded would come to life right here before me, in two human rows staring plaintively at me? Tears came to my eyes. I remembered Amersouda's kiss on the unwritten regards, and I spoke:

"The boat was leaving and I did not have time to write down the regards for all of you that Amersouda was begging me to write. She has not forgotten anyone; she remembers you all!"

The old woman pulled back her pitch-black kerchief and her face reappeared, smiling this time.

Translated by Yianna Liatsos

In the Old Catholic Syros

Kostas Ouranis

SYROS, SEEN FROM THE SEA, is like a superb water-color. Two conical peaks, covered from their roots to their tops with white, pink, and blue houses, are reflected in the calm water.

These two peaks are two different worlds.

One is a new city, Ermoupolis, that at one time appears to have justified being named after Hermes, since it was a large mercantile and seafaring center. It has wide straight roads, large symmetrical houses, and a large, stone-paved square, where in the afternoons the high society of Syros gathers to hear the Philharmonic play old operas and to see and be seen. It is an attractive city in a state of decline. Its maritime and mercantile activity is of no consequence today. Most of its stores along the waterfront, which in the evenings are lit up with multicolored lights, sell nothing but *loukum*. Syros *loukum* is so famous that all the travelers on the various ships that stop here consider it obligatory to disembark in order to buy it as a gift for their relatives.

In the new city live the Orthodox. Its hill is crowned by a Byzantine church, whose white cupola shines against the blue of the sky. For a century, this church was a refuge for

Greeks during disaster: first the people of Chios fleeing the fires and slaughter at the hands of the Turks and later the Greeks of Asia Minor filled its courtyard like a flock of frightened doves. Today, its sunlit yard has that great religious calm that transcends place and events.

On the other peak, to the left as one sails into the port, is the old city. It is crowned by an ancient Catholic cathedral that dates back, they say, to the time of Louis XII. When the traveler Tournefort visited he called it "the most Catholic city in all the archipelago." The same is true today, but that doesn't mean much any longer. There was a time, however, when Catholicism knew days of great glory in several of the islands of the Cyclades: the time of the Crusaders and of Venetian sovereignty over the sea. The great families with unusual foreign names that put down roots in the islands were all Catholic. Those islands were their fiefdoms. They had large fields, they were rich, and they had power. Today, of that prominence, the descendants of the great Venetian families have nothing left but their memories. By the time Comte de Gobineau visited the islands, the Franks, as the Venetians and the Genoans were known, had fallen into decline. In his charming novel *Akrivie Phrangopoulo,* Gobineau shows us the descendants of the Franks trying to preserve dignity in their poverty, something that is both touching and comic. They despised the people, who returned their sentiments in kind. Having wangled from a great power the unsalaried position of vice consul, the former aristocrats would await the chance arrival of some foreign warship so they could make official visits, lending each other faded frock coats suitable for diplomatic occasions. Today, displaced by a smart and enterprising Orthodox petite bourgeoisie, these property-less descendants have nothing left but empty titles and the big, rundown ancestral houses, almost bereft of furniture, which they keep open from a residual concern for dignity, hardly fooling anybody, including themselves.

As a descendant of one such great family in Santorini asked sadly of a British traveler, "they say, 'We are great families and we must have big houses.' But for what reason?"

This small Frankish community constitutes a separate world. It is the ghost of an epoch that has passed. During a visit to one of the islands of the archipelago, I came across the house of two highly placed Catholic priests of that area. The two of them were the personification of the decline of that alien religion in the small world of the Cyclades, the mortal remains of a bygone past. Their faded black robes and the dark blue velvet caps on their heads had something pitiable about them. Seated close to each other on the sofa, they resembled two rag dolls, with the stillness and the set expressions of such dolls. One was smiling vaguely as if lacking all reason, like a harmless madman. The other rested his head on his chest and dozed. Their appearance was somehow both melancholic and ridiculous. As I looked at them, it seemed to me that if they got up to leave it would be to return to the past as ghosts.

The whole Catholic quarter of Syros has that same air: of having been extinguished and existing outside the present. Whoever wanders through it does not see the noisy bustle of life; very few people go up and down the little streets and the endless, tiring steps. Perhaps you may see an old Catholic priest in white robes disappear into the glare of a narrow, deserted street, or a peddler prod his miserable donkey before him, not even hawking his wares. Once in a while two or three women with red pitchers pass like shadows from the Bible. The silence and the alternation of light and shadow in the steep and winding roads, and the old whitewashed flat-roofed houses, reminded me of the Casbah in Algiers, where the sun burns like a furnace but the shade has the coolness of a cistern. This part of Syros is just like the Casbah except that it lacks the Eastern mystery, the silhouettes of the women with covered faces who appear for a second in the opening of a window, and the blind reclining beggars, with eyes that resemble egg whites, who sing their lament near the fountains. Here there is no mystery whatsoever, only the great peace of stagnation, which only the light prevents from being mournful. Cats yawn before the doors of the houses; flowers decorate the old, dilapidated walls. Through half-open gates you may glimpse a courtyard with a grapevine and, hanging from it, a cage with a twittering canary. Now and then you pass beneath a room that bridges two houses, or by a little house at the point of collapse with picturesque wooden loggias that remind you of Italy.

Ascending the hill you pass from one such picture to another. At the summit there is a different kind of calm. Here the peacefulness does not have the same character of somnolence and fatalism. It is light-drenched and timeless. The panoramic view from the summit changes your perception. From above, the entire Catholic quarter seems to flow downward toward the sea. Your eye embraces the descending terraces of flat roofs, steep-stepped roads, stone-paved courtyards, and microscopic gardens enclosed by stone walls. From the hill you can see across to Pyrgos, the highest peak of the island, grooved by ravines that trickle down in small streams and feed the old fountain in the city where the women gather to fill their jars. Rows of cypresses mark the positions of the cemeteries, where the dead of both faiths sleep. And below, the sea spreads out its boundless calm surface, flashing with golden rays. On the horizon of the sea several islands appear suspended in the mist, Tinos, Mykonos, and, farther on, Delos, alone and forgotten by life.

Some say that Syros has no natural beauty. Others praise the beauty of Della Grazia, the countryside where the wealthy residents go to vacation. As a rule I don't believe in prevailing opinions, and Syros, more than any other place, justifies my disbelief. This famous Della Grazia is a countryside that has, it is true, some greenery, a thing quite rare on most of the island, but the pompous villas that the wealthy residents have built are in lamentable taste. With their garish colors, their turrets and their statues, they make an area ugly that without them would have been simply ordinary.

Contrarily, I fell in love with the old Catholic Syros, which is dying quietly under the shadow of its old cathedral—looking out on a sea that the ships of the Venetians and the Genoans no longer cross. Its beauty is not simply the melancholic and paradoxical beauty of death, which is imprinted as much on people's faces as on objects. The old city creates a touching antithesis to the mercantile and nouveau riche contemporary city. It reminds me of the aged faces of noble ladies whose faded features preserve the traces of incorporeal beauty and in whose melancholy gaze one may glimpse distant visions of grandeur. In the evenings, when the lights on the quay of Ermoupolis are lit and one can hear the sounds of the phonographs and people are strolling on the stone-paved square, the old Syros remains silent and almost dark. Perhaps there was a time when the life of the new city filled it with jealousy and bitterness. Today, however, the old city seems to show only the supreme indifference of people who, without having yet died, no longer belong to life.

Translated by Catherine Siskron

My Home

Melpo Axioti

IN THE DELOS ISLANDS, the crows are going to sleep —which is to say, it's almost dark. From the beginning of the world this exodus has been going on: whenever it's about to get dark the crow clan sets off en masse for the waters of Delos. They spend the night on those two rocky little islands. But for their regular work, during the day— foraging to unearth some dead animal or other, or what you

Editor's note: A book written in political exile, *My Home* brings to life the author's native Mykonos and uninhabited neighboring islands, Delos and Rinia. Its view of the islands is one that no visitors could discover on their own. For while antiquities on Delos and windmills, beaches, and whitewashed buildings on Mykonos attract obvious attention, their stories remain unknown. In this excerpt, Axioti chronicles the islands' history from the perspective of scavenger crows that forage on Mykonos during the day; a patient donkey that hauls goods from villages to countryside; and the windmills, built to make Mykonos self-sufficient but destined to draw the curses of church officials, governors, and an American wishing to acquire property in Greece.

might call those orphan cats and dogs that wash back and forth in the foam on the beach, or swooping suddenly into Frosso Gryparenas's courtyard to snatch her thimble or any other shiny thing, because the crow's lineage is of the thieving kind—all this they do on the capital of the Delos group of islands, which is Mykonos, where they spend their days.

A long-lived bird, the crow; in all its infinite life, it has this same journey to remember, day and night. But on one single occasion, in those deserted hollows, on those peaceful nights, a man appeared to disturb them: Dimitris Stavropoulos. Overseer of Antiquities for the Cyclades, he had read—it was toward the end of the last century—his Thucydides and he saw it there in writing, that the Athenians declared Delos to be sacred ground, and not only was it forbidden for mortals to be buried or born there, but they dug up the graves, in the year 424, to remove the bones and whatever else was in them, so as to take them across to Greater Delos, which they called Rinia.

And now Dimitris Stavropoulos was about to do this business again: dig up Greater Delos, disturb the peaceful birds. Because he needed to find "the cess-pit scouring" there. And what jewelry, what vases, what pots he found in that awkward trench, what plates and saucers, an oil can, a lamp, things from the rich or the poor household, its collection of ornaments that are a necessity to the living, for they must go together to the underworld. And large and small, they were found in tiny pieces, the pieces of broken glass made a mountain, although the educated person would never call it glass in smithereens, but rather "shards."

All these shards and similar antiquities that they carried from Delos had various consequences. At some point they had thrown a slab into a cellar that was an annex of the school. One day a small Mykonot named Yiannis Svoronos happened to be put there under lock and key as a punishment. How was he to spend his time, his punishment time? He looked at the slab, felt it with his fingers, saw an old inscription written on it. But at the moment when he read it, he didn't know that he was carrying out his very first piece of scientific research. Because he didn't yet know that he would become a renowned archaeologist.

And the other consequence of his "cess-pit scouring" brainwave were that the overseer Dimitris Stavropoulos, remained written in history, the island acquired its important museum, Greece enriched its collections, humanity supplemented its knowledge of ancient civilizations, and the Mykonot tailor Polykandriotis, who became a restorer, went blind, his whole life bent over the pots, gluing them together.

The crows may head for Delos, but the donkey stands thoughtfully near Pouloudhis's bakery. He stands so still you'd think they had promised to make a statue of him. And for all that he's in a real hurry. Darkness caught up with them when they were still in the fields, and for his part, he can't see in the dark. He's not some sharp-eyed rabbit. And his master, Nicholas, will be pushing him to make it to the village, so add another hour, fully loaded, even if it's a donkey doing the walking. "Heh, giddyap, you brute!" he'll say to you. But how can you speak to him, answer him back, say, "Why were you running late, eh? Is it my fault now?" OK, so when we're racing back, I hope Nicholas gets his balls caught in those big slabs of rock! It's a long way, brother, even if you're a tetrapod, with these four feet. And a weak constitution, your youth passing, your haunches fallen, and you're almost out of breath.

Listen, there are other places where they have horses, fat buffalo, huge sloppy things, but in this place they've only got mules—to be a companion and provider of food for your master—and this small-framed creature, a mere slip of a thing. If some visitor from far away should happen to come by, he'd stand and wonder, he'd laugh. Such a knowledgeable animal, he'd say in his head, but to spend all day turning the press for the melon field, with his eyes blindfolded to keep him from getting dizzy, and carrying all that stuff on his back, from the villages to the countryside and from the countryside to the villages. And brother, there are so many villages, such a horde. An odd lot these people! "Where are you heading for, mate?" you say to him. "I'm going to my village," he tells you. And by "village" he means just his house! OK, he might have a little bit of a garden beside it for the vegetables, a scrawny vine or two, because the mildew keeps rotting them (it's not the way to grow them), but this thing, if you have it, this holding, this lot, such places are a long way off. You've got quite a distance to go! By the time you've reached Abourdehti, Linos, Linaria . . . And houses are scattered between them—house and village. Just sit and count them now! You see, the folks who live here found plenty of room, with no sort of fancy building work getting in the way; they just took it and spread out. Dried-up countryside, stone on stone, rocks and precipices, so they've got you squeezed between land and sea. Where's the milk going to come from to make some cheese, since there's not a flock of goats or sheep to be seen on the rocky heights of the island? Where's the little bit of feed to be found, that you must not eat, you've got to sell it so it can be sent off to the cities, where it'll be a good advertisement for your village. Rocks and precipices.

They eat human bones; first measure your strength carefully, then tackle them!

But more than the philosophy that the thoughtful donkey was considering now, tied up like that—and had there been no rope, he would still have stood there without moving because he knew his business—he was calculating the delay. As soon as Nicholas came, oh my! How he'd race him home! Without a single stop. There'd be no time even for a piss.

It's the season for pennyroyal. The whole place is covered with it along the road. The sweet smell of it will make your wide nostrils twitch, but you'll be aware again of that tang of piss that the earth makes a hollow for, right there in the middle, and you'll stop and the boss will wait respectfully so you can get on with it. Hey, it can't be just anywhere! All the creatures smell it from way off and hurry to come and relieve themselves. But should it happen, one time, that a whole lot of tetrapods find themselves together, they'll form a line, to relieve themselves as a group—even if it's a scorcher, or pouring with rain, or windy, the mule-drivers will stop patiently, until the convoy starts moving again. But now, with this delay, ugh! But for God's sake, let Nicholas get here fast!

When you leave the village for Anomera the first hill you climb on your way is always the one with the mill, Pentaras's windmill. The lone one. A crow that crowns the crescent of the shore. Because most of the mills, the ones in a line, those stand on the summit somewhere else, over Alefkandras way. They stand on the hilltop, as if they were about to start grinding.

Long be their lives like this one's! Bones more aged than

a donkey's. Covered in wounds. Some wing came here to be plucked or fall out. There hangs the frayed grassy beard of the roof; its face has turned the color of deep rust. Another one stood there forever, a little further over, the small door shut tight even if the wings are outdated, or the belly formed by the wall is all swollen. When the moon goes down, if someone should pass by these despotic fat bodies, with their arms wide or with their backs cut off at the roots, in the ghostly light of the moon he may feel some fear: could it be a fairy, or did they hide contraband in here? And he would tremble. But the one-eyed mill beckons from its high window. "Come, come and don't be afraid," it tells him: "courage!" while the chickens run boldly up to him, scratching to find stray seeds before they manage to sprout.

People talk, they always talk. The mills were built. People always say that. But no one really knows for sure just when the mills were built. It was in times when there was a lot of business. Plenty of grain. It had to wait its turn to be ground. When one of those things called progress came, that was when the furious ballyhoo of the mill first started slowing down. They had brought in the little machine. It stopped for good when they brought the big machine. Then you saw only the business of foreigners, in a hurry, coming here to look at things. What was there to look at? And what did they understand about such things!

So, now, the mill was brave. It gathered its strength to bear its final misfortune: the foreigner's tread. Never in its life has it heard of some Don Quixote colleague, a fairytale lie of how the mill lives and reigns even with plucked feathers. There are still people around who have seen the slow death of the Mykonot windmill. The children always run and study it, as if the ancient presence is sitting on its heavy body, like when you search for old traces in the veins of the earth. From its youth until today, such a lot of things have happened! What discoveries, what cries, what hopes! But it is deaf—like bygone times that move on without fail. Only just recently word got around that an American is looking to buy it, and in order to save it he's going to turn the mill into his own house. "Four thousand dollars." The American hears—and is horrified. He figures how much he's prepared to spend, to lay out a bunch of money for a round box! It's not as if it were really necessary! He's probably heard they are going for nothing, old wrecks like that. The Greek earth is full of them, you can just pick one up as a souvenir.

And there ends our knowledge of the American. But old Mrs. Beatrizo, who taught us: "If it weren't for what came before, would there be anything now? And whatever might come afterward?" That's why, compatriot mill, I try to keep on living: so as to preserve you.

Remember that period when you were not wounded and you ground the wheat? It was the time of Turkish oppression, with the harsh laws, the forced labor, the Greek fleet sailing the Aegean. There was need and to spare—the fleet had to be maintained, it had to be fed, the sick needed beds. One island, Paros, undertook the building of the hospital and escaped the plague; so for the Mykonots to escape it too—writes one investigator—"they must also contribute to this building, as quickly as possible, they must cut two thousand wooden beams, two and two and a half *orgias* in length, an inch wide, and two or three fingers deep so as to construct the roof. This forced labor was terribly oppressive, driving the unfortunate islanders to ruin. The orders

were not infrequently accompanied by threats." And curses
—as in this letter of Patriarch Gerasimos of Tyrnavos to
Mykonos—in the year 1674.

From, † Gerasimos, by God's mercy Archbishop of
Constantinople New Rome, and Ecumenical Patriarch

To, † Most Reverend Archbishop of Sifnos, beloved
brother and fellow-worshiper of the Holy Spirit,
esteemed members of the clergy, and most devout
priests and leaders of the island of Mykonos, may the
Grace and Peace of God be with you!

The most noble and gracious wife of the late
lamented Panayiotis, Madame Perouzes, has
informed us that on the island where he lies at rest,
income from the past year has remained uncollected,
income which the omnipotent sovereign deemed
should be received by the widow's orphaned child to
be used for necessary expenses. Regarding this
income, she has appointed as guardian of her child
the very estimable Mr. Fotios, who has arrived there
with the express purpose of assiduously gathering the
income of the preceding year and delivering it. . . . If
you should fail to submit and comply and do not pay
the income for the past year, let those among you
who are clergy be suspended from celebrating all
sacred mysteries and rites and let them be deprived
of their income and parishes. . . . As for the laymen,
let them be excommunicated by Almighty God, let
them be cursed and their sins unforgiven, and let
their bodies not decay and liberate their souls now

and for ever after their deaths, for wood and iron will decay, but they, not at all. Let them inherit the leprosy of Uzziah and the gallows of Judas and let them not prosper by God's grace as long as they live; let them be cursed by the Nicene Fathers and all the remaining saints of the three hundred and eighteen Holy Synods and let them be outcasts of the Church of Christ, neither attending Mass nor receiving blessings nor being worthy of burial after death while under the penalty of their suspension. Thus we have decreed and let it not be decided otherwise. May the Grace of God be upon you all.

1674 in the month of June of the 12th Indiction.

† Jeremiah of Chalcedon, † Anthimos of Athens,
† Gerasimos of Bizya, † Makarios of Derka,
† Cyril of Prousa

In these Turk-trodden years, together with these curses, the terrible threats, you also had to grind, mill. But you had a big problem: you could not grind. You stood idle, mournful, your wings tied, and you didn't know that the Mykonot syndicate was sending the following piece of paper to the central authorities—to defend you. Quite a few years have gone by now: a hundred and ninety-one. For it was written on the twentieth of March, 1772:

The sirocco has dominated the weather now for four months and with such winds these mills cannot operate. The majority of the inhabitants use a hand mill to grind the flour they eat. Consequently, if the northerlies don't start blowing, there won't be any flour. And again we have wheat from the other store, 500 kilos of grain that Captain Vasilis's *Andros* unloaded, and loaded the marbles of Delos; they left it here for us to make flour from, and that remains unground too. And that together with what all of you other Greek regions have sent us makes a total of more than 200 kilos; and may the northerlies blow soon here so that some of this may be ground. The heat of summer being on its way, the grain may dry up and spoil in the warehouses and you should be aware of it.

But it's not only you, mill, that they harass, making you grind without any wind. There are also the Mykonot sailors. And her boats. They want to take them away from her. Worse than your troubles, this one, since "the boats rule this island," as it is written.

Esteemed and worthy shipowners and compatriots who find yourselves over there in Constantinople:

We send brotherly greetings to your honors and ask God to grant you good health. Now we must inform you that on the one hand we were gladdened by the eighty sailors that you write to us they no longer require, but we are making you aware of the fact that the Sultan's Naval Commander came to us in his cutter and showed us an official document asking us for eighty men in addition to our ships. That is why we are sending the bearer of this letter, Antonakis, and for this purpose we are writing to the

Lord Dragoman and to His Excellency the Naval Commander and *Arji Hali* of our master, Captain Pasha, and having read the requests, you will understand what we tell them and we beseech your honors as compatriots, together with the bearer of this letter, to make every effort concerning this affair, so that we do not come to any harm, because, as you know very well, it is the ships that rule this island, and you are quite aware that this coming of the ships to Constantinople will bring so much harm to the place and complete ruination; but we had hoped that greater mercy might be shown to us in such times and that we would not be asked independently for both sailors and ships. It is not necessary for us to beg you because we know that you are even more eager than we, and may Holy God grant you health, and finally we bid you all farewell, hoping to rejoice in your good health as is our fondest wish.

1769 February 21

Your loving and ever-eager, Mykonot Municipal Community

And whatever expenses accrue concerning this case, the present Mykonot Community undertakes to accept them all.

And seventy-four signatures follow.

Translated by Gail Holst–Warhaft

The Smile from the Abyss

Manolis Xexakis

DOWN IN A GLEN I KNOW there is a round ossuary where women come down and wash the heads of the deceased with wine on Saturday of the Souls.

My mother has my grandfather there, too, and she visits him.

They bring the skulls down from the display cases, they carry them to the yard, and they lay them down on the side wall.

The scene can give chills to an innocent passerby.

This whole business happens in the morning, the time when the day is lighting up and a murmur sprinkles through the olive trees as do drops of sun.

It can pull your heartstrings to see the harmonious figures of living bodies plant themselves by the bare bones in that deserted place.

They go and pour wine in copper buckets and then, carefully, softly, without dipping their fingers in the black holes, baptize the skulls for a long time and "caress" them. They say, "My ill-fated one, my unfairly killed one, once upon a time you were a human being too . . . ," and as the sun rises for good, the priest arrives and reads the prayers over a plate full of memorial wheat, and as soon as he is finished the women talk among themselves about those who have left but are still present.

By noon they all leave the cenotaph and the area withers completely.

From stories, I hear that my grandfather was shot in his eighties.

The Germans surrounded the village and rounded the people up. They brought them down to a ravine with their hoes on their shoulders, and the interpreter kept telling them that they would be transported to the airport at Tymbaki for work. The captives spent hours in anticipation. The wind was blowing with sudden swirls, then it would disappear.

The procession of the morning frost was passing before their eyes.

They had been arrested in retaliation for someone in the village who had disinterred two dead Germans so he could take their boots and clothes.

The Germans separated the women out. They arranged the men in a line. They made them dig the graves. A few shots were heard from a machine gun, and then the dull finishing shot.

Later the women went as far as the ravine to the open graves, where they cleaned the bodies of the dead and covered the ditches, without a cross or writing or any special sign.

After three years they each identified the heads of those shot by the final gunshot hole in the skull.

But even now there is one skull that three women claim and they do not know exactly to which of the dead it belongs.

So on Saturday of the Souls all three wash and clean the skull together, and each believes that it is her loved one.

Well, in this treacherous world there are dead who belong to all of us, and we must all claim them.

Otherwise souls are stuck in the thorns and human deeds blown away by the wind.

Translated by Anastasia Koumidou

Black and White

Rhea Galanaki

For M. G. Parlamas, teacher and scholar

SHE SAW HIM ON THE HORSE outside the antebellum coffeehouse in an unknown village. Smiling, he had relaxed his body and the reins slightly, so that he and the horse would appear proud on the plaque. His doctor's bag hung from the saddle. It was summer, it seemed, for he was wearing a brimmed straw hat with riding gear, high black boots, and a white, long-sleeved shirt. He was staring into the distance, perhaps in anticipation of the notorious revolt that was about to break out (the failure of which led to his imprisonment and subsequent flight to France) or perhaps because this was the pose the times demanded. The same horse had galloped over his rainbow: over the dark colors of the war and money lost—dark blue and purple; over the sky blue, red, and the yellow colors of home and family; over the green color of mourning; then it had stood firm on the final color, the pale orange of memory. She put her palm on the horse's neck to hold the last intact. With this as reins, she set out to do what she had avoided for years. She opened the gate, mounted the horse, and left home.

They proceeded to that part of the waterfront where she

remembered a few benches and weeds. The stone parapet had been built on the crumbling walls, not so high that it would hide from the benches the view of the sea and the promontory opposite, the purple mirror of lovers that reflected the transparency of their thoughts as they crossed the blue waters of the bay. Sometimes there was just the echo of words divinely inspired and old, winged words that exist only as waterfowl. Atop the horse, she stood next to the benches, a meeting place for high school couples. The road she remembered behind the waterfront was narrower, without cars, and for this reason newly paired couples would come down to stare at the deep blue of adventure. She let the horse lower its head to smell their adolescent bodies. She offered a silent tribute and, without dismounting, observed the unchanging, liberating view. Now at this height she could see more clearly not only the deep azure blue but also the adventures that followed. Then she lowered her gaze to where she could see the rocks with their brown seaweed and sea urchins. She saw her own face, too, twenty years younger, leaning down, trapped in a different hairstyle, fearful of the height and the inhospitable crag and—what at the time she had intuitively sensed but could not yet identify—of the police.

Despite the drone from the cars on the road, despite the din from the wall of apartment buildings, hotels, and restaurants, all newly built—though two blocks of conclusive silence sweetened the noise, one with half-standing Venetian facades, the other with that abandoned neoclassical house of some obstetrician (how many times she had dreamed of living there, not because it was one of the few neoclassical buildings in the city, but because it was the only house that faced the sea, ignoring the city's triangular, immured inwardness)—despite the noise, then, she was able to hear the shattering sound of the water breaking on the crags, as if she could feel the water itself. Though water, especially water, never remains the same, its shattering sound filled her stomach with broken crystal and frightened flowers. The horse shuddered, startled by the noise of glass inside her, a fragmenting image. Or maybe it was startled by the persistent summer wind that scattered papers on the road and forced her to hold onto that old-fashioned hairdo with both hands, to lift her face from the photograph.

Iraklion, first stop, she noted on the back of a white sheet of paper. The city has overcome the sea. I think I heard the water mourning its imprisonment. Mourning its youths.

She had gone up the road many times by foot or car but never on horseback. A constant and very real sense of danger from the cars pressed her as far to the right as possible, so that she was practically on the sidewalk. She was growing more tired as she went on, for she had to stop regularly to observe the faces of passersby—and it was not easy for her, watching from the friendly height of the horse, to distinguish any feelings other than curiosity in their dark eyes. Once or twice she sensed that someone recognized her. It was not the eyes that gave this away but the hint of a smile that never became a greeting, for the reality of twenty intervening years warded off recognition. This reality did not differ significantly from an assumption that death had intervened. Nevertheless, on top of the horse she had a better view of the store and office interiors. Storekeepers would regularly come out from their shops, lawyers and civil servants from their offices, to light a cigarette and watch silently. The very few who didn't smoke would fan themselves with a half-finished contract or their local morning paper. For the day was beginning to heat up even on that road, which lay to the north and therefore had often been the scene of wonders from the other side of the sea that entered city life like native ritual processions.

She led the horse up on the sidewalk. The mournful boom of the bass drum shook her insides as it passed, sounding the beat for the slow march of scouts, students, soldiers, and priests. The band director was holding a long baton tied with blue velvet ribbon and gold braid. A spear from the war museum? Not even that, perhaps the mystery of the music itself. He raised it and spun it in the air. The wind instruments started to play. The horse pricked its ears toward the shrillness. Next in line were the cherubim and banners, then the sacred object of worship carried among flowers and the priests clad in gold from head to foot. As they shifted their weight rhythmically from one foot to the other, they all forgot that they were dancing once more the most ancient, somber dance. She waited for them to move away toward the waterfront, then returned to the street.

If the street was often transformed into a long, narrow, linear stage, this was because the city's buildings provided the backdrop as they preserved memories of a grand urban architecture with scattered Venetian landmarks. Carved cornerstones, stone arches, and cantilevers gradually found their places in the scenery, as if a cracked plaster garland or the fragmented Serenissima Lion suddenly defiled memory in the ruins. And if some rituals (especially those involving water) were still enacted in the street and the whole city came down to view them, signs indicate that the upper floors of the scenery housed business offices or hotels, while the ground floors housed travel agencies and souvenir shops.

The blue disappeared as she left the waterfront and neared the fountain and the bright, fruit-strewn market-place. She stopped the horse. Water defined her departures and returns, a blue ritual. This was where she used to come to buy tickets for the ferry—she was at a loss to understand how ancient people and places crossed paths irrationally on the timeless sea until she realized that this was the sea's last defense against summer's foreign languages, whereas the crossings had begun purely for profit. This was where she used to buy tickets for the ferry boat that sank—perhaps because it had not been given an ancient name, so that somehow it had resisted general liquidation before it sank, something that took on pagan dimensions after its loss.

She had enjoyed traveling on the boat that later haunted her sleepless nights. She led the horse over the wooden decks, past wooden chaises longues, wicker tables, crimson couches, white curtains, and gatherings of friends from her first undergraduate year. They used to return for the holidays or summers and would pass the whole night on the boat talking until very late, sometimes daybreak, if the dark rocking of the sea did not put them to sleep. For until that time the sea had been the road that led to Piraeus of the morning light, with its mysterious atmosphere of dock lights glowing until day took hold, with few human souls or cars except for the longshoremen and taxi drivers, with its briny morning air, the hurly-burly of anchors and mooring lines, and especially with the promises of a freer life. Freedom seemed indistinguishable from those scenes of a half-asleep harbor observed through a round screenlike porthole. And when in the next year freedom sank with the ship, her friends gave it a coarser, more visionary definition, and they changed their lives.

She was not at all surprised when the horse took her to a coffeehouse at the end of the road and stopped outside its open door. The coffeehouse once had served local passengers on long bus rides before filling with blond, half-naked angels from foreign lands. Bright light emanating from either them or the sun forced her to shade her eyes with her hand as she leaned slightly to study the pale yellow paint on the walls. She was searching for the black hull that plied the gray seas of a photograph—like a fly on a framed glass pane, its own sea of death—next to the kitchen counter between clay copies of the Prince of Lilies. For it happens that some old items left behind in coffeehouses (either through superstition or inertia) bear witness to—or rather create—a myth. She loved these items so dearly that she was willing to put herself at risk for them—as she was doing now, for she entered the coffeehouse, moved toward the photograph, removed it from the wall, took it into her possession, and retreated, all on horseback though she threatened to knock glasses and cups and saucers from the tables. Without a word about price, the coffeehouse keeper followed her to the door, wiping a glass with a cotton towel. And when she turned back for a moment in leaving, afraid to look at him, she realized that he was much more frightened than she, for the hands on the clock had turned back to show darkness and waves. There they stopped forever.

Iraklion, second stop, she wrote on the frame's beige paper backing. Here the theater of hope was always linear. The ship Iraklion sank under its own weight. No friend survived unharmed. Friends grow fewer in numbers.

The museum garden smelled of chamomile and pine, just as it had the day the poet's funeral began there. She dismounted the horse and stood under the umbrella of pines in the corner as the procession again passed by, muted and dimly lit, since sound and color wear away with time.

She had spent many long hours in that garden learning to love the small fragments that once had been feelings. It was usually cool and empty, the museum garden—if you could call a garden the few pines and benches that faced the sparsely peopled ocher hills and the city's first factories, if you could call a garden the foreground of an African lithograph, with its chimneylike brick palms, pale, dim light, and bare trace of Mediterranean blue in the upper left-hand corner. If it was indeed a garden, it owed its garden character to the coolness brought by the museum dead, rather than its high location or the persistent summer winds, for the dead bring a cool feeling to town museums.

The horse rubbed its nose in the dry grasses, pleased that miracles still occurred so that it could be left in peace —for now the museum guards and tourists had suddenly petrified, in order to allow memory to twist about like the octopus painted on the belly of a Minoan pot. Memory thus turns on miracles. In the same way, the faces of closest girlfriends petrified, though she could still distinguish in the black-and-white film of their faces the love that fanned the flames of adolescent monologues. The garden was the confessional of girlfriends, where even the most Platonic of loves spoke or was spoken of in words from old novels or old epics filled with strict parents and disobedient daughters.

Twenty years' absence had transformed the words of adolescent loves into golden honeybees and papyrus blooms in the low glass display cases. Or was it the height of the horse or the reflection of its face and of her outline in the museum display glass above the words that made her hear them again as the horse walked slowly now from room to room, its hooves echoing as if it were wearing golden horseshoes? Certain acquaintances who no longer worked there smiled and waved at her, as if they had been thinking about her just so during her absence. She waved back and bent down to look at the scratches and cracks in the words. Suddenly she understood why they had talked about love in the museum garden. There all the lovers of Knossos were long dead, but they stood by the girls like angels with whatever little things they had salvaged or that had preserved them. There the words of love remained indecipherable on the Phaistos disk, something that made love a mystery or a game but never a self-evident truth. There, too, the decision of some friends from the group to take the university entrance exam for archaeological studies signified an erotic approach to death, typical of their romantic adolescence, she thought, except that at that time they had not yet been able to understand. She guided the horse out the door to avoid the modern scene.

Iraklion, third stop, she wrote on the back of the photograph. The memory of smells, the distant echo of words, the reasons for decisions that were right at first, all survive. The garden is different.

The horse was thirsty. She led it to a street opposite the museum entrance and found herself in her old school yard.

She had never before noticed that in summer, schools resemble watercolor paintings, for forgotten running water diffuses the outlines so much that everything seems to swell with the summer wind or a sigh. She had never before noticed that spirits occupied the school yard, especially at summer's midday; or perhaps the water was to blame when she saw the spirits smiling, gathered in the middle of the yard as she turned from the fountains. She caught the reins to assure herself that this was not a dream and just managed to hold back the horse, which was ready to flee, trampling on the photographs with their curled edges, since it thought her suspicion was fear. She calmed the horse, then guided it gently to the rectangular shadow of the wall.

At the center of the yard the sun evaporated field trips, parties, school prayer, secret journals, the peculiar amorous atmosphere, the Sunday walk, movies, recesses, the first pair of nylon stockings, the first demonstrations, the end-of-the-year play, songs on the radio, boys who attracted her, feelings for teachers, the walk to school with her brother. Her desire to leave forever. Sadness and happiness, the only interpretation of black and white.

Sophocles' Antigone appeared, eyes filled with tears from the joy of recognition, shining brighter and larger on a face shrunk to minuscule size from the merciless perspective of time. "Black-and-white shades of death," she whispered.

But this was a different death from the symbolic one of the ship or the distant one of museums. Here adolescents who fell in love met their fate. Now they were destined to wash their face in the school fountain all day so as not to hear the clock of St. Minas. They would remain forever youthful and sinless.

The girls' dark uniforms and the boys' school caps were dripping wet. They were wiping their faces with their palms —faces full of expectation for her future. Their modest, carefree movements revealed that they all recognized their death twenty years ago. They also knew, however, that they would remain connected to her through unbroken if illusory bonds of a certain time and place, because this was the nature of old feelings. They tried to guess the life they had lived since that time as they silently looked each other in the eye. It became clearer that many counted tenderness in numbers, and this—was this all?—this made them unable to remember the name of the one who had committed suicide, the ones in jail, the one who had lost his mind, though these things had occurred after graduation, or even the name of the girl who had miscarried in the middle of class. They confided in her that they had practically forgotten how to write. How could they remember the names of those sad souls when they could hardly remember their own—when they couldn't recall a single line from Lorentzos Mavilis's poem "Oblivion," whose version of the happy dead they embodied? They reminded her that what was not written down was forgotten.

The horse brought her to the gate as it carefully crossed through tender shadows. It was leaving the labyrinth just after the slaughter, and the burden of winning would not allow victory to beget pride. For this reason her body was not dripping with the blood of the monster. Drops of water were streaming down to the horse's happy hooves. She understood that she and the horse were being washed in the fountain's cool water even as she left the labyrinth, winding slowly the bloodied spool of memory's thread.

The clock of St. Minas struck two from the marketplace. School dismissed. She was glad, not that she had conquered death but that at last she had learned that there was no punishment in summer school yards, where those lost in the loneliness of their dreams met and reconciled. She had also learned that there was no evaluation of their afterlives, which they have not yet begun to live even though they have reached its midpoint. The absence of latter-day judgment still encouraged school daydreams. In the language of spirits, this meant their peculiar death, where dreams of a future life on earth constituted the heaven and hell of their motionless pose.

She picked out one photograph and wrote on the back: Iraklion, fourth stop. Water washes away the sins of praise and of time. I have found no other way than feelings.

The cuckoo popped out of its door and told the time in the kingdom of the forest: two in the afternoon. Then she heard her mother calling her for the midday meal. She placed the photographs on the table in the living room and watched the horse's orange color escaping through the open window. After eating she would smoke a cigarette and then study the pictures filtered through the distance of a nicotine high. How was it that for a moment as she descended she thought she saw the stairs, the highboard, certainly the cat, and the set table in black and white?

Late at night, she will see her friends again—the hour when the sea becomes silent, black with white shirts on the dock and lamps hanging in rows—and search in the rose garden of human colors for the angelic black and white of lightning-speed contacts. No one will wound with winged words the bones of the Minotaur on our empty plates, as this text begins to leap up before us, forever black ink on white paper.

Translated by Artemis Leontis

Kalymnos

Margarita Karapanou

KALYMNOS IS A MELANCHOLIC ISLAND, strange and mysterious. In the streets you see old men and women with black scarves and sad faces, sad looks, tired gaits, bent backs. They have lost their sons to the spongeries, to the dives that bring death along with those priceless sponges or, even worse, leave them paralyzed. Now, fortunately, this tragedy is over. The diving equipment has improved. Sponge diving today is much safer. Accidents don't happen anymore. The young men can go down to the depths to gather sponges without the same dangers.

I remember, many years ago, the first time I went to Kalymnos. There was a rough sea and I couldn't take the regular boat that goes from Piraeus to Kalymnos. I had to take an airplane to Kos—I am terrified of planes. . . . In Kos there was a horrible wind, and after a flight when I was sure the airplane would crash I arrived in Kos, with the wind sweeping everything to and fro. They put me up in a disgusting hotel, in a room with a mattress full of fleas. In the next bed a very polite policeman was sleeping—it reminded me of my novel *The Sleepwalker.*

At around three in the morning the boat finally arrived,

and they told us to embark. It would take us to Kalymnos. The winds must have reached almost hurricane conditions. Usually with such winds it is forbidden to sail. The captain shouted some nautical terms that I didn't understand. He kept shouting "shit" and "fuck" until, with great difficulty, the ship moored at the pier. We boarded by a ladder that consisted of a few planks and two ropes to hold on to. "Get in quickly, folks, we're going to sink!" the captain shouted. We stepped onto the sparsely arranged planks, which shook from the stormy sea splashing us up to our waists. I was trembling with fear. It was three in the morning, February, the coldest month of the year. It was raining waterfalls. Night. We couldn't see a thing out of the portholes. All we heard was the terrible sound of the rain pitilessly pelting the ship. We felt the prow of the ship dive deep into the huge waves and then finally emerge, like a drunk, like Rimbaud's "Drunken Boat."

An old lady jumped into my arms and clung to my neck. "I'll never see my son again, the one who went to Australia. I'll never see him again. He's coming back tomorrow to Kalymnos, and we, my child, will be swallowed up by the sea tonight in this rotten wreck. Maybe it's Saturday of the Souls? Oh, God, at least my soul will see my son and welcome him. And then our souls will be reunited after death."

"What's your name?" I asked her.

"Mrs. Aryiro. I am a pastry maker. Kalymnos makes the best *galaktoboureka* in the world, my child, and mine will drive you crazy: lots of butter, lots of cream; our *galaktoboureka* swim in butter. Come tomorrow to the harbor to our store and eat a whole pan."

And though I felt terribly nauseous from the unbeliev-

able swaying of the boat, my mouth got all watery in anticipation. I am a total glutton. The nausea got mixed up with
my appetite for a whole pan of *galaktoboureka*. The old lady
and I fell asleep in each other's arms.

When we arrived in Kalymnos, my friend was waiting
for me. I didn't see any of the island, just like when I crossed
New York City in a truck with my eyes shut because I was
afraid of the heights and the skyscrapers. It was the same
with Kalymnos: I didn't see a thing that first night, such a
long time ago now. I went to my friend's house, fell into
bed, and slept for twenty-four hours.

The next morning I went for my first walk. It was driz-
zling. The island was melancholic, remote, as if it had been
forgotten by the rest of the world. A mist hung over the sea,
which was now calm as oil. It looked like a lake. I went
down to the harbor. It was full of cafés and bakeries. I went
to Mrs. Aryiro's shop and ate a few pieces of *galaktoboureka*.
I drank a glass of cold water. Motorcycles were racing
around giddily. Even before I had gotten to the harbor I
had seen them racing through the back alleys doing wheelies. I heard an old fisherman near me say that many kids
had been killed from such stupidity and carelessness. My
desire to leave Kalymnos became harder to control.

I caught a cab and said, "Take me to see a view, if there
are any." We left the harbor, passing by incredible beaches
with deep black stones eaten away by the sea, beaches that
looked like volcanoes. The sea was deep green. The sun had
come out. All at once I fell in love with Kalymnos. We
drove up into the mountains. We saw the sea from up high
sparkling in the sun. We passed by countless beaches.

In the afternoon we went back to the port. Again the

same melancholy, the sad wrinkled faces of the women. Again the strong desire to leave Kalymnos, to leave now, immediately. The sea had gotten rough again. There were no boats, not even the little ones that take you to Kos. My relation with Kalymnos was and remains even now strange, like a love affair. Contradictory and paradoxical, at once hate and attraction. All the time I was there, one minute I wanted to leave, the next I wanted to stay forever. When I think of all the places in Greece, only Kalymnos brings on such emotions. Greek landscapes are transparent, clean. They inspire peace or awe or happiness. Epidauros arouses a sense of awe, the Cyclades unbelievable joy; they are prosperous islands. But Kalymnos is a melancholic island. It is the island of sponge divers and of poverty. The young people, back then, went diving in the deepest waters to find the biggest, most valuable sponges. Often they either died or came out paralyzed. It is the island of terror. Their mothers wore black clothes, black scarves on their head, and grew old before their time. It is and remains the island of departure and separation: the young boys leave with the ships to seek their fortunes elsewhere, to come back to the island rich, to help out their family. They'll make fortunes. But at what a cost. They drown growing older like Odysseus on his never-ending wanderings. . . .

The fifth day I left as if I were being chased. Such an irresistible urge to leave. I didn't even wait for the big boat that came later. I took the small one to Kos and felt that I had been rescued from a terrible fate. . . .

Translated by Karen Van Dyck

Astradeni

Eugenia Fakinou

TODAY'S AN IMPORTANT DAY for me. I'm going to my
new school, my Athens school, which I'm sure is fantastic.
It simply can't be that all these kids here aren't going to super
schools. After all, one doesn't live in Athens for nothing.

On Symi our school is built of dressed stone and has a red
tile roof. It's also got a triangular pediment with a circle in
the middle. By the gate with the wrought-iron patterns
there's a carved stone that says, "31st August 1876." That's
how old our school is. It's so old, it's almost lost the pebble patterns in the pavement of the yard. The children's feet
wore them out over the years. So many children, so many
years, the poor pebbles simply wore away and vanished.

But we've created garden plots all around the yard, and
each class plants its own plot. And because the plots are big,
we divide them up among class groups. Stamatia, myself,
Irene, and Thareini were the third group in my class. Only
it was the onions that fell to our lot. That is, Ma'am drew
lots and said, "The first group will plant broad beans, the
second group small lilies (the lucky ones!), the third group
(that was us) onions (Disgusting! We couldn't have done

worse. And they don't even produce a flower), the fourth group will plant chickpeas."

But the sixth year, the older ones, had all the luck. Tsambika's aunt, who lives in Athens, sent her a packet of seeds for flowers called "sweet peas." She brought some to school and sowed them on the very edge of the plot. In the spring they produced the most incredible flowers in all sorts of colors, and we were all crazy about them. We gathered the seed (it looked like peas) and this year we sowed them all around the garden.

They'll blossom in May but I won't get to see them, seeing that I'm now living in Athens. Oh, heck! What's come over me? After all, I'm not going to cry just 'cause I won't see the school sweet peas in blossom. That would be the end! I bet there'll be thousands of flowers at the Athens school. They're bound to have the most beautiful and the rarest ones.

Mother combs my hair: the part in the middle and two identical braids with red clips at the tips. My school smock is washed and ironed (when did she iron it without me noticing?) and the collar in place. My school bag, the crisps, are all ready. My bag is red, white, and blue. White is the pocket on the front. Maria, who now lives above us on the second floor, had sent it to me from Athens. All the girls were green with envy. On that white pocket there's a girl and a boy kissing. They're kissing because the boy's a seaman who's come back from abroad and found his fiancée again. No one's told me this; I've just thought it up myself.

Father searches his pockets to make sure he's got the

paper from the Symi school. Maria's late, and I'm so anxious. Suppose I get that dragonish teacher. Maria rings our bell three times. Mother makes the sign of the cross over my head and kisses me.

Maria's waiting for us at the door. She says, "Oho, that's quite a schoolgirl!" and we're on our way. She says she's coming with us as a witness that we really live at this address. Because, she says, many lie about living in this neighborhood in order to send their children to this school. And because the school's got too many children, they have to check carefully. You take along a water or electricity or phone bill to prove that you're really living at the address you give.

Fancy that, they don't believe you, and you must show them papers. And because we have no papers, we'll show them Maria who's got papers and they know her. Funny business this, and complicated too. In Symi you go to school just like that, with nothing. Never mind, this is Athens.

We come to a very broad street. There's a hospital here too, a very big one. It's three floors high and all glass windows.

"Here we are," says Maria.

I'm stunned. Is it possible they lied to me about taking me to school in order to take me to a hospital? They know I'm scared of doctors and hospitals and they've tricked me this way. But then why the school smock? Could it be this isn't a hospital but really a school?

"It's very big," says Father, impressed.

"Sure," says Maria, "eighteen hundred children go to

school here. Three different schools are housed in this building. We must find out which school Astradeni belongs to and the times she'll be coming."

I'm speechless. Fancy eighteen hundred kids and three schools together. And how am I to know which is *my* school? How am I to tell it apart? And my class, which one'll be my class, and how am I going to find it? Fancy, eighteen hundred children!

On Symi the entire school was sixty kids. And the other school at Yalos had about a hundred. There were eighteen of us in my class, and the third year, that was next door, was sixteen kids. Classes were taught by twos. The same teacher taught the third and fourth years together. While we were writing an essay, the third year took dictation. When the third year had history, we did copying of text. We sat two at a desk, one row of girls' desks, one row of boys' desks. I sat with Doukissa at the third desk. In front sat Stamatia with Irene, behind them Irene and Alemina, then me and Doukissa, and behind us Maroula and Vasoula. The boys were all sitting in the next row of desks.

What girls am I going to sit with here? I wonder.

We walk in. The whole school is painted gray. It's really like a hospital; I can't get over that idea. There's a high railing around it that gives you the feeling you're penned in. They've got a thing here in Athens about fencing kids in: chicken wire on Maria's balcony, high railings round the school. Very odd.

We cross a very big yard. Sure, it's for eighteen hundred kids, after all. But where are they? I can't see a soul. We come to a passage.

"You wait here, Astradeni," Father says. I grab him by his

trouser leg. I'm not going to be left alone here. It's full of passages and doors and eighteen hundred children. I'll get lost; I'll lose my father.

"I'm not letting go of you," I say.

"All right, you can wait outside the Head's office." The Head's office! So this is the Head's office. If I lean over a little, I can have a peep. I can see some chairs covered in leather and another door beyond.

I sit down in a hurry, 'cause a door opens somewhere. A little boy runs past me like a shot and asks, "Have you been sent out of the room?" but doesn't even stop for an answer. From somewhere I hear a lot of kids reciting in unison, "The unstressed ah"—on the "ah" they raise their voices— "on the ultimate of the imperative of verbs is lo-ong."

Father comes out of the office with Maria and a gentleman. Could that be the Head?

"Well, Astradeni," says Father, "you belong to the 26th Primary School. You'll be having morning classes from eight to one Mondays, Tuesdays, and Wednesdays, and afternoon classes from two to seven Thursdays, Fridays, and Saturdays. This gentleman is the school's caretaker and he'll take you to your class. Lessons have started already. I'll come for you at one o'clock, okay?"

Father bends over me with his hand on my back.

"Okay?" he says again.

Yes, I nod. He's told me everything all at once, and I'm all mixed up.

"Come along," says the gentleman called the caretaker and walks ahead. I take a few steps, then turn around and look at my father. He waves to me. Tears are coming to my eyes.

Where am I going? As long as I have my parents beside me, I'm not scared of this strange place. But now I'm on my own. It's one thing to be alone on the island, and another thing here. It's more scary here.

Well now, Mistress Astradeni, what's the idea? Are you going to burst into tears for the new teacher to see you in such a state as to form the wrong first impression? So pull yourself together, perk up, and follow that gentleman they call the caretaker.

We stop in front of a door. It has three signs on it:

26TH PRIMARY SCHOOL, CLASS E3
30TH PRIMARY SCHOOL, CLASS E4
31ST PRIMARY SCHOOL, CLASS B1

Okay, then, this is my class, the E3. I must look for something to help me find it again. Well, we'll see. Now the gentleman opens the door and pushes me in gently.

First thing I see is Ma'am. I can't tell whether she's young or old. She's got her hair pulled back into a tight knot and wears glasses.

"What is it, George?"

"A new girl, Miss."

So she's "Miss," not "Ma'am." She's not married, though she's no spring chicken.

"And of all the classes they chose to send her to mine? I've already got sixty-two in here. Never mind; thank you, George."

I'm standing somewhere near the teacher's desk. I look at the classroom. It's large, yet it's full to bursting with kids. There are four rows of desks. At most of them there are three kids. And there are two more desks next to the teacher's desk.

"Find a place and sit down," says Ma'am.

Two girls are sitting at the third desk in the second row. They look likable and I walk toward them. But by the time I've got there, they've slipped to either end of the desk and pretend not to see me. What do I do now? Do I say, "Move over"? No, I can't. I look around. They all pretend to be looking into their exercise books, but I know they're watching me. What do I do?

I heave a sigh. Further along there's another desk with a free seat. A boy and a girl are sitting there. I go over. When I get to them, they too have moved to either end of the desk. I look around, uncertain what to do. I hear some giggles. They're doing it on purpose. They don't want me to sit next to them, but why? I must have gone red as a beet. I turn and face them. I wish I could disappear into the ground. I'm just standing there with a hard lump going up and down my throat.

"Haven't you sat down yet?" asks Ma'am from her desk. What shall I say? That they're making fun of me?

"Come and sit at one of the desks along the side," she says. There are two desks placed sideways under the window. The front desk is occupied by two girls and a boy. A boy's sitting alone at the desk behind.

"Sit with George who's on detention. The rest of you can finish your dictation."

I sit down. George looks me up and down but says nothing. He isn't taking the dictation. I put my bag on the desk and wait. I don't know what I'm supposed to do, so I watch the teacher. She's wearing a gray skirt and jacket, and shoes with low heels and laces. They're gray too. She's busy with something on the desk. George sees that I'm looking at her, gives me a little shove with his knee, and then takes hold of the point of his collar, giving it a good shake. I know this gesture means so much as "the teacher's a real harridan." I pretend to pay no attention and keep looking straight ahead. Come to think of it, this George could be young Kyriako's cousin. Sure he is, for he's on detention too. Except I don't know the teacher's name.

The kids seem to have finished their dictation, because some girls get up, collect the exercise books, and take them over to the teacher.

"Now," she says, opening a green book, "you, the new girl, stand up and tell me your name."

I stand beside my desk and say, "Astradeni Hadzipetrou."

Ma'am isn't looking at me. She's about to write my name in the book (it must be the register), but the kids start laughing, I don't know why. She raises her head, strikes the desk with a ruler, and says:

"Quiet, you lot! What did you say your name was?"

"Astradeni Hadzipetrou."

"Hadzipetrou sounds right to me, but Astradeni, is that a *Christian* name?"

I nod "yes" with my head. I'm shaking. It seems she doesn't like my name.

"Do you mean to say this is the name the priest gave you at your christening?" she asks again.

"I was christened Asterope, but they call me Astradeni."

"And Asterope, is that a *Christian* name?"

"Yes, Ma'am. Our Ma'am, my teacher, I mean my old teacher, told me it's a very ancient name. It's one of the seven stars of the Pleiades."

What's come over me that I say all these things? There you are, the kids are laughing; they're laughing their heads off in fact.

"Quiet!" shouts the teacher striking the desk with her ruler again. "I know of no such name. But never mind; when's your saint's day, so I can make sense of all this?"

"There's no saint's day for Asterope; I've only got a birthday."

More laughter from the class. But why on earth are they laughing like this? I must try to patch it all up somehow, or else this teacher will put me on her blacklist.

"Some girls called Asterope, Ma'am, celebrate their name day on St. Urania's day. But I have no name day."

"Well then, to get this over with," says Ma'am and writes "U-RA-NIA HA-DZI-PET-ROU" speaking out each syllable.

"Asterope, Ma'am!" I cry. "That's my name."

"You watch it now, because you and I won't get along if you go on like this! I'll call you Urania, which is a name in accordance with our church, and that's that."

"But Ma'am . . ."

"Miss, not Ma'am. From which school have you come to us?"

"From the Chorio School on Symi."

Nothing could hold the kids anymore. But what the devil, may God forgive me, have I said again to make them laugh like that?

"All right, you may sit down now. Well, let's see, all of you who are giggling. Do you know what Symi is?" asks the teacher. They all fall silent for a while. Then a girl raises her hand and says it's a town in Euboea.

"Not *Kymi* but *Symi*," says Miss sternly—I must get used to this Miss, Miss, Miss.

"Well then, tell us, Hadzipetlou, what Symi is, since the class doesn't know it."

"It's one of the Dodecanese islands," I say.

Then we open our reading books and talk about all the poetic elements in the assigned text. Miss asks Petropoulou, who seems to be her pet, to give me the timetable and tell me what exercise books I must keep. All this during break, of course.

In a few minutes I hear the bell ring. It's very loud. All the kids run out of the classroom. More kids from other classrooms tumble down the stairs. You'd think thousands of horses are stampeding.

George is allowed no break, since he's in detention. Petropoulou and another girl come up to my desk. Petropoulou has blond hair held to one side of her head by a silver clip. Her school smock is very neatly made and has got a lace collar. She's wearing white socks and beige shoes with a strap across the instep. She looks very neat and clean. The other one must be her friend. She's chewing on a doughnut, and there's sugar stuck all around her mouth. George has covered his face with his hands as if he's sleeping, but I'm sure he's listening. Petropoulou reads out the timetable to me day by day, lesson by lesson. I'm writing it down saying yi-es, yi-es, so she can go on. At some point she stops reading.

"If you say 'yi-es' once more, I'll drop everything and go. This peasant accent of yours is getting on my nerves."

I feel a hot wave rising in my face, and my eyes grow dim. I guess I'm blushing. Good Lord, what have I done wrong again?

"What's wrong with saying 'yi-es'? How else am I to say it?"

"Well, well, get this true native of the capital," George mumbles. "And since when, if you please, has Levadia become the capital of Greece and I didn't know it?"

"Don't think I haven't heard what you've just said," Petropoulou cries angrily. "Maybe my dad came from Levadia, but my mummy's an Athenian. Yes, indeed! And my grandpa, if you really must know, was an officer in the army."

She's really mad. She starts off on all sorts of yarns, about her grandpa whom the king summoned to his presence and said, "Save the Fatherland from danger!" and about her mummy who's the most beautiful mummy of the whole class. Her friend keeps nodding all the while, as if to confirm it's all exactly as Petropoulou says. George pretends to be snoring very loudly, and this annoys her even more.

The more I look at her, the more I think Petropoulou's like Sotiria, except that this one is blond. She tells me what exercise books I must keep, too. Most of them are the same as we had on Symi. I only need to get a GENERAL one, she says.

The bell rings. The kids come in and we have religious instruction. I know the chapter "St. Paul in Prison," as we'd already done it on Symi. We were five pages ahead in the book.

The bell rings again. This time I go out, too. The yard's full of kids, really full. The big boys are playing football. The girls are walking about in groups. The youngest kids are running around like mad; they tear past you, they hide behind you.

I locate the water taps. At the other end of the yard, on the right, there's a long trough with many taps. Even so you must queue up to get a drink of water, that's how many kids there are. As I'm standing there behind a little girl, I hear someone say, "Asteria's come to have a drink, too," and the other girls giggle at the joke. I don't care, let 'em say whatever they like. Let 'em laugh all they want. I'm not even goin' to turn around and look. I don't know who she is; I don't want to know. I have a drink of water and walk on alone, just like that. Then I see a little glass house in the middle of the yard. The kids come up to the open window and buy things from a man. And what all don't they buy! Chips, crisps, chocolates, waffles, orange drinks, sweets, chewing gum. Where on earth do they get all the money? They buy two packets at a time; the school must be full of rich kids.

The bell rings. It's very loud and can be heard coming from all directions. We stand in line. I haven't lost sight of Petropoulou. Wherever she went, I went. So I found my class and stood at the end of the line.

We march to the classroom to have a history lesson. We were eight chapters ahead of them on Symi.

Just before school's out, Miss says we're to bring fifty drachmas tomorrow. On Saturday we're going to the museum. A museum in Athens! Well, sure we've got a museum on Symi, but the Athens Museum must be something fantastic!

On Symi they tried to collect everything old that was still around in the houses: island dress, lace, crochet work, painted or carved chests, weapons, bracelets, coins, silk embroideries, copper coffeepots. They added all the ancient things and the old icons and so put our museum together. It was very neat. For a building they took the Hadziagapitos house up at Chorio and renovated it.

In the courtyard, among the pots of marigolds and basil, they set up some big ancient pieces of marble. In one room they have ancient potsherds on display. In other rooms are the icons and the weapons.

But the best job was done in the big room. The walls are still covered with the pictures that were originally painted on them: little angels, pink and green ribbons, flowers, fruit. The ceiling is painted all over, too. Between the mirror and the chests they've set up big dolls wearing our old island dress, the everyday one as well as the fur-trimmed one. They've got a male doll too, in the breeches of old times. The first time I went in, I thought the dolls were alive. When I realized they were dummies I was disappointed. Then I imagined them talking to each other in the evenings, or on days when the museum had no visitors. they'd walk about, eat out of the soup terrines placed nearby, and live a secret life of their own. Actually, the one in the fur-trimmed dress was in love with the man, that's how I imagined it. But the man wanted the other one, the one in the everyday dress. Then the one in the fur-trimmed dress thought the reason for this was the moth-eaten crochet work round her scarf.

That's why in the night, and without the other two noticing, she went to the next room and stole a beautiful piece of mauve and green crochet work. So it's the one in the fur-trimmed dress that stole the crochet work and not a tourist, as the guards thought. And she wears the stolen piece when the guards are away, so they won't realize she's alive.

They could really be alive, if they wanted to, those dolls in the museum. There's everything there a household needs except food. But dolls don't need any food. And in the evening I fancy them going out into the yard and gazing through the arches at Yalos below with its electric lights and the music from the taverns and shaking their heads as if to say, "There are so many things we left too soon to see and to experience, really."

I thought, too, that maybe in a hundred or two hundred years me too, I might be a doll in the museum. I might be wearing my school smock or my yellow jacket with the ducklings, and my hair braided, and people would be walking past looking at me and saying, "How beautiful girls were *then!*"

I'd be hearing them, but my eyes would be staring straight ahead without moving. Yet in the evening I'd be walking with the other dolls in the yards and on the terraces gazing at Yalos from above.

What might we be seeing then, a hundred or two hundred years from now, I wonder.

I wait till the kids and the teacher have gone before I leave the classroom too. In the yard there are only a few boys now playing football. Father's standing at the gate. He asks me how I got along in the new school, and I just say, "Fine," what else. Or should I tell him that the teacher will call me Urania to make a Christian of me, or that they're making fun of me and I could find no place to sit; or that "yi-es" had got on Miss Petropoulou's nerves. I only tell him I need a fifty-page exercise book and fifty drachmas, because we're going to the museum on Saturday.

Translated by H. E. Criton

Contributors

ARTEMIS LEONTIS, adjunct professor of Modern Greek at Ohio State University, has published essays on Greek literature in Greek and English. Her book, *Topographies of Hellenism: Mapping the Homeland,* which studies Hellenic ideas of place, was named outstanding academic book for 1995 by *Choice* magazine. A recent fellow of the National Endowment for the Humanities, she lives and works in Columbus, Ohio, but continues to explore the Greek world through literature and travel.

∽

ELLI ALEXIOU (1894–1988), born in Iraklion, Crete, worked for most of her life as a teacher. She took an active role in the Greek resistance to the Nazi occupation during World War II. She lived in self-imposed exile in East Germany after the Greek Civil War until 1962, when she returned to Greece. She wrote novels, short stories, and a biography of Nikos Kazantzakis. Her work expresses deep empathy for the marginal elements of Greek society.

MELPO AXIOTI (1906–1973), born in Mykonos and raised in Athens, was one of the first Greek authors to explore in fiction the fragmentary nature of identity and memory. After publishing *Difficult Nights* (1938) and *Do You Want to Dance, Maria* (1940), two modernist novels, she wrote chronicles in the socialist realist tradition. She moved to Paris in 1945, when the French government gave fellowships to selected artists and intellectuals who had resisted the Nazi occupation in Greece. She was later expelled to Eastern Europe because of her Communist convictions. Axioti wrote *My Home* (1962), her last prose work, in Warsaw and East Berlin, completing it shortly before she fulfilled her ardent desire to return to Greece.

YIORGOS CHOULIARAS (1951–) was born in Thessaloniki. He studied in Oregon and New York City, where he has been living since 1975. He has published several collections of poetry: *Iconoclasm* (1972), *The Other Language* (1981), *Treasure of the Balkans* (1988), *Fast Food Classics* (1992), and *Letter* (1995). English translations of his poems have appeared in many literary magazines, including *Poetry, Grand Street, Mediterranean,* and *Modern Poetry in Translation.* Chouliaras is a "postmodern" Greek author whose writing undermines received notions of national identity.

GEORGIOS DROSINIS (1859–1951) was one of a group of authors who introduced the anti-Romantic realist techniques of French Parnassianism to Greece in the 1880s. Throughout his long life Drosinis published many collections of poetry and prose. He also wrote scholarly essays on literature and folklore, was managing editor of several important newspapers and journals, directed a museum, and worked in the Ministry of Education. His writing is characteristized by a simple, clear, and playful style, even when it treats the heavier philosophical issues that interested their German-trained author. Drosinis found inspiration in contemporary Greek history and the traditional life and customs of the rural population. Typically, his stories narrate events from rural life with precision and careful attention to plot.

ODYSSEUS ELYTIS, the pen name of Odysseus Alepoudelis (1911–1996), was born in Iraklion, Crete. He studied law at the University of Athens, but devoted his adult life to writing. His first collections of poems, *Orientations* (1940) and *The Sovereign Sun* (1943), helped introduce surrealism to Greek letters. *Heroic and Elegiac Poem for the Lost Lieutenant of the Albanian Campaign* (1946) draws on his experiences as second lieutenant on the Albanian front in the Greek-Italian War. Elytis represented Greece in international congresses of writers and art critics in Europe during stays in France in 1947–52 and 1969–71. His epic poem *The Axion Esti* (1959), set to music by Mikis Theodorakis in 1964, earned him the First State Literature Prize for Poetry in 1960 and paved the way for the Nobel Prize for Literature, which he was awarded in 1979. Elytis's poetry has been widely translated.

MICHEL FAïS (1957–), born in Komotini, studied economics at the University of Athens. He has worked as an editor, critic, journalist, and writer for newspapers, magazines, and television in Athens. He is currently overseeing the creation of an archive of audio-recorded interviews with authors. Faïs published a collection of poetry, *The Border*, in 1983, and a novel, *Autobiography of a Book,* in 1995 (translated into French in 1996), which brings together a decade's worth of research and writing. A recurring subject in his work is the presence, history, and cultural contributions of Jews in Greece.

EUGENIA FAKINOU (1945–), born in Alexandria, Egypt, grew up in Athens. In 1974 she learned the art of the puppet theater in Belgrade. She opened her own puppet theater in Athens in 1976 and illustrated children's books before turning her attention to writing adult fiction. She received rave reviews for *Astradeni* (1982), a novel about an eleven-year-old girl whose family leaves a close-knit island community on Symi near Rhodes and moves to Athens for economic reasons. Five novels have followed. A common theme in Fakinou's work is urban middle-class consumer culture that gradually displaces regional folk traditions and leaves people uprooted.

RHEA GALANAKI (1947–), born in Iraklion, Crete, studied history and archaeology at the University of Athens. She now lives in Patras. She has published poetry and prose: *Albeit Pleasing* (1974) and *The Minerals* (1979), both collections of epigrammatic poems; *The Cake* (1980), *Where Does the Wolf Live?* (1982), and *Concentric Short Stories* (1986). Her two complex novels are both inspired by historical figures: *The Life of Ismail Ferik Pasha (Spina nel cuore)* (1989), the first Greek novel ever included in the "UNESCO Collection of Representative Works," and *I Shall Sign "Louis"* (1993). A book of essays is forthcoming this year. The short stories in *Concentric Short Stories* weave together personal and collective memories of Crete as they recall a past invisibly tied to the narrator's consciousness.

Galanaki's prose is carefully worked, musical, and dream-like. Her poetry, short stories, and first novel have been translated into several languages.

MARIOS HAKKAS (1931–1972), born in Pthiotida, grew up in the Athenian neighborhood of Kaisariani, to which his short stories have brought fame. Throughout the Nazi occupation, this district was the symbol of Greek resistance, marked by the blood-stained events of the *Skopeftirio* (shooting ground) where at least a thousand partisans lost their lives. In 1950 Hakkas volunteered to go to Yaros, an island of political exile, to help care for political prisoners. His studies in political science were cut short by a four-year imprisonment for his political views. During a brief span of seven productive years he wrote some of the finest short stories that appeared in Greece after World War II. His best-known collections are *The Bidet and Other Stories* (1970) and *The Commune* (1972), written as he was battling terminal cancer and at the same time struggling to develop a clear, ironic view of modern urban Greece.

DIMITRIS HATZIS (1913–1981) was born in Ioannina a few months after the end of its five-hundred-year Ottoman occupation. He grew up to see great changes in the rugged, mountainous northwestern region of Greece, where many languages were once heard and a large population of Greek-speaking Romaniote Jews lived until World War II. During the war, Hatzis joined the resistance to the Nazi occupation, about which he wrote in his first novel, *The Fire* (1946). His involvement in the Greek Civil War ended in his flight to Eastern Europe, where he lived as a political refugee for twenty-five years. A leading postwar prose writer, Hatzis focused on Greece's fast-changing provincial towns rather than the villages or cities more commonly treated in prose works. In Bucharest he published *The End of Our Small Town* (1953), a collection of stories about Ioannina. The clash of a traditional economy and modern industrial society is a theme in Hatzis's *The Double Book* (1976), too, referred to as one of Greece's first postmodern novels.

YORGOS IOANNOU (1927–1985) was born in Thessaloniki, the son of refugees from eastern Thrace, now part of Turkey. He grew up during World War II in Jewish neighborhoods, where hunger and mass execution were constant threats. He worked as a teacher. He wrote many "prose writings," as he called them, atmospheric pieces usually set in Thessaloniki and told in the first-person voice of a sensitive, restless outsider. The tone blends critical observation with the personal confession. Ioannou's prose collections include *For the Sense of Honor* (1964), *The Sarcophagus* (1971), *The Sole Inheritance* (1974), *Our Own Blood* (1978), and *Epitaphios Threnos (Burial Lament)* (1980).

MARGARITA KARAPANOU (1946–) grew up between Athens and Paris, a daughter of the celebrated Greek author Margarita Liberaki. She has written three novels: *Cassandra and the Wolf* (1974), *The Sleepwalker* (1985), and *Rien ne vas plus* (1991), of which the first is her best known both at home and abroad, having been translated into English, French, German, Swedish, Dutch, and Hebrew. *The Sleepwalker* received a literary prize for the best foreign book in France in 1988. Themes that recur in her writing are schizophrenia and the merging of fantasy and reality.

NIKOS KAZANTZAKIS (1883–1957), born in Iraklion, Crete, is one of Greece's most world-renowned writers. He grew up during the Cretan uprisings against Ottoman rule, then studied law in Athens and Paris. He traveled widely. He wrote poetry, drama, and travel books on southern Greece, Russia, China, and Japan. Although he considered *Odyssey: A Modern Sequel* his major work, that epic, which comprises twenty-four books and 33,333 lines and took up the adventures of Odysseus after the slaughter of Penelope's suitors, did not bring Kazantzakis critical acclaim. Instead he is best known for his seven novels, which he began writing late in life so that he could "let off steam," as he said. They are *Zorba the Greek* (1946), *Freedom and Death* (1953), *Christ Recrucified* (1954), *Last Temptation of Christ* (1955), *God's Pauper, St. Francis of Assisi* (1956), the posthumously published *Fratricides* (1963) on the Greek Civil War, and *Report to Greco* (1961), an autobiographical novel.

CHRISTOFOROS MILIONIS (1932–) was born in Peristeri near Ioannina, Epirus, in northwestern Greece. He studied classics at the University of Thessaloniki and began publishing short stories in the 1950s. He was a member of an editorial group that published literary journals in Ioannina in the 1960s and 1970s. He has written short stories, novellas, novels, and critical essays. His collections of short stories include *Akrokeravnia* (1976), which refers to a mountain range in Epirus, and *Kalamas and Achéron* (1985), a cycle of stories that take place where the river Kalamas meets the Achéron, the mythical boundary between life and death. That collection won him the Greek State Literature Prize in 1986. His stories record memories of Greece's bloody decade of war, from the Greek-Italian War

(1940–41) and the Nazi occupation (1941–44) through the Civil War (1945–49). Milionis's work has been translated into English, Russian, Italian, German, French, and Hungarian.

KOSTAS OURANIS, a pseudonym for C. Niarchos (1890–1953), was born in Constantinople. He studied in Athens, Paris, and Geneva. He traveled widely as Greek consul, secretary of the Ministry of the Press, and a journalist before settling in Athens in 1924. He wrote many articles and books on his travels. His symbolist poems, written in formal patterns that match the themes of memory, nostalgia, and escape, greatly influenced Greek poetry of the 1920s.

ALEXANDRA PAPADOPOULOU (1867–1906) lived most of her life in her native city of Constantinople, where she supported herself by teaching and writing. She briefly taught in Bucharest and was principal of girls' schools in Thessaloniki and Selymbria, a one-time Greek city on the Hellespont. She published one novel, *Diary of Miss Lesvios* (1894), and more than 150 short stories. She was interested in portraying the lives of women from the Greek urban middle class. She excelled in dialogue and in the detailed observation of manners. Papadopoulou's short stories were collected posthumously in 1929. They have never before appeared in English.

GEORGE SEFERIS, pen name of Yiorgos Seferiades (1900– 1971), was born in Smyrna in Asia Minor. He studied law in Athens and Paris. In 1926 he entered the Greek diplomatic service, which took him to London, Albania,

Crete, South Africa, Egypt, Italy, and Ankara in various posts; he served as Greek ambassador to Great Britain from 1957 to 1962. He wrote many collections of lyrical poems, including *Turning Point* (1931), *The Cistern* (1932), *Mythistorema* (1935), *Log Book I, II,* and *III* (1940, 1945, 1955), and *Thrush* (1947). He also distinguished himself as a literary critic, translator, and writer of essays. His acquaintance with the poetry of the French symbolists Valéry, Rimbaud, and Laforgue and the American T. S. Eliot was decisive. A tone of nostalgia is characteristic in his poetry and prose, which often evokes the reality of a past event, a myth, or a state of mind as it focuses on a real landscape — typically an ancient site. In 1963 he was awarded the Nobel Prize for Literature, the first Greek to earn that distinction. He received honorary degrees from the universities of Cambridge, Oxford, and Princeton.

THANASSIS VALTINOS (1932–), born in the Peloponnese, is internationally known for his novels, short stories, plays, and film scripts, many in collaboration with Greek film director Theodoros Angelopoulos, including the award-winning script of *Voyage to Kythira* (Cannes Film Festival, 1984). His innovative work has earned him numerous awards, such as the Greek State Literature Prize in 1989 for his novel *Data on the Decade of the Sixties*. Valtinos's prose relies on the power of oral and written testimony, which he considers to be both an authentic, persuasive document of the visible world and a filter of a complex, indescribable reality. Stories remain in a "raw," uninterpreted chronicle form. Subjects that interest him are the anonymous participants in Greece's recent political and social upheavals of the twentieth century. His work has been translated into French, German, Swedish, English, and other European languages. His own translations of classical Greek drama are performed at annual theater festivals throughout Greece.

VASSILIS VASSILIKOS (1934–) is perhaps the best-known living Greek prose writer at home and abroad. Born in the northeastern town of Kavala, he grew up in Thessaloniki, where he studied law. Since 1959 he has lived in Athens, New York City, Rome, and Paris. English-speaking readers may recognize him as the author of *Z* (1966), a novel about the politically inspired conspiracy surrounding Gregory Lambraki's death, which Costas Gavras made into a blockbuster film. Vassilikos is a prolific author who has written on a wide range of subjects. A recurring theme is the asphyxiating condition of modern life, but Vassilikos's innovative genius has given this a wide variety of forms. Also translated into English are *The Harpoon Gun* (1973), *The Monarch* (1976), *Outside the Walls* (1973), *The Photographs* (1971), *The Plant, the Well, the Angel: A Trilogy* (1964), and . . . *And Dreams Are Dreams* (1996).

ILIAS VENEZIS (1907–1973), born Ilias Mellos in Aivali of Asia Minor, chronicled his captivity in a Turkish compulsory work camp in *Number 31328* (1931), his first novel. He escaped to Athens in 1923. His novels include *Peace* (1939), *Aegean* (1941), *Winds* (1944), and *Hour of War* (1946). He wrote several collections of stories and a play. He also wrote travel essays on many parts of Greece. The theme of Greek refugees from Asia Minor recurs in his prose, which follows a realist tradition. Venezis has been widely translated.

EVA VLAMI (1920–1974) was born in Piraeus to an old aristocratic family of Galaxidi. She studied music in Athens, but became known for two prose works, *Galaxidi* (1947) and *Skeletovrahos* (1949), both of which chronicle the history of the once wealthy and important port that lies west of Delphi. Vlami's writing follows an "ethographic" trend in Greek prose, which concentrates on describing the manners and customs of traditional rural life, though she was conscious that the world she described was already nearly eclipsed in the 1940s.

MANOLIS XEXAKIS (1948–) was born in Rethymno on the island of Crete. He studied physics at the University of Thessaloniki. He has published several collections of short stories, including *The Death of the Cavalry* (1977), *Mathematical Problems* (1980), and *Amorous Sailings* (1980). His stories treat the themes of love and power. They resemble dream narrations intended to exorcise a painful memory without, however, blotting out the trace of history.

LEONIDAS ZENAKOS (1932–) was born in Athens. He received a degree in classics from the University of Athens. He has published two books of poetry, *Tenaro* (1955) and *Springs* (1962), as well as some prose pieces, and has translated ancient Greek drama for the modern stage. He is currently managing editor of *To Vima*, the leading Sunday newspaper in Greece.

Permissions

continued from copyright page

Vassilis Vassilikos's "The White Bear" is reprinted from . . . *And Dreams Are Dreams,* a novel in seven parts by Vassilis Vassilikos, translated by Mary Kitroëff, published by Seven Stories Press, © 1996 by Vassilis Vassilikos. Reprinted by permission of the publisher.

Marios Hakkas's "The Fresco" from *Apanta (Complete Works)* © 1972 Marika Hakkas; English translation © 1997 Gerasimus Katsan. Translated and published by permission of Kedros Publishers, S.A., Athens.

Odysseus Elytis's "Funerary Epigrams" © 1992 Odysseus Elytis; English translation © 1997 John Chioles. Translated and published by permission of Ikaros Press, Athens. Quote on page 29 is from Pindar, *Fragmen*t 124, 7; and Pindar *Pythian Ode* 4, 131.

Nikos Kazantzakis's "Pilgrimage Through Greece," translated by Peter Bien, is from *Report to Greco.* © 1961 Helen N. Kazantzakis, renewed © 1993 Helen N. Kazantzakis. English translation © 1965 Simon & Schuster, Inc. Reprinted by permission of Simon & Schuster, Inc. and Kazantzakis Publications, Athens.

Ilias Venezis's "Mycenae," translated by Nicholas Kostis is reprinted from *Modern Greek Short Stories.* © 1944 Ilias Venezis; English translation © 1993 Nicholas Kostis. Reprinted by permission of Odysseas Publications, Athens.

Thanassis Valtinos's "Panayotis" was originally published in Greek in the collection, *Tha vreite ta osta mou ypo brohin: digimata (You Will Find My Bones Under the Rain: Short Stories)* by Thanassis Valtinos. © 1992 Agra Publications and Thanassis Valtinos, Athens. "Panayotis" first appeared in this English translation by Jane Assimakopoulos and Stavros Deligiorgis in *Deep Blue Almost Black: Selected Fiction* by Thanassis Valtinos and published by Northwestern University Press in